INTRODU

The Freud Wars

Stephen Wilson and Oscar Zarate

Edited by Richard Appignanesi

ICON BOOKS UK   TOTEM BOOKS USA

Published in the UK in 2002
by Icon Books Ltd., Grange Road,
Duxford, Cambridge CB2 4QF
E-mail: info@iconbooks.co.uk
www.iconbooks.co.uk

Published in the USA in 2002
by Totem Books
Inquiries to: Icon Books Ltd.,
Grange Road, Duxford,
Cambridge CB2 4QF, UK

Sold in the UK, Europe, South Africa
and Asia by Faber and Faber Ltd.,
3 Queen Square, London WC1N 3AU
or their agents

Distributed to the trade in the USA by
National Book Network Inc.,
4720 Boston Way, Lanham,
Maryland 20706

Distributed in the UK, Europe,
South Africa and Asia by
Macmillan Distribution Ltd.,
Houndmills, Basingstoke RG21 6XS

Distributed in Canada by
Penguin Books Canada,
10 Alcorn Avenue, Suite 300,
Toronto, Ontario M4V 3B2

Published in Australia in 2002
by Allen & Unwin Pty. Ltd.,
PO Box 8500, 83 Alexander Street,
Crows Nest, NSW 2065

ISBN 1 84046 381 3

Printed and bound in Australia
by McPherson's Printing Group, Victoria

Freud's Origins

Sigmund Freud was born into an unprosperous Jewish family in 1856.
His place of birth was above a blacksmith's forge in Freiberg, N. Moravia,
at that time part of the Austro-Hungarian Empire. He was talented,
ambitious and wanted to become famous.

Freud's childhood hero was Hannibal, the (Semitic) Carthaginian
general who fought the Romans.

A 20th-Century Landmark

Freud longed to become a successful medical researcher and make important discoveries. But academic medicine did not pay a living wage and he lacked private means, so he reluctantly trained in Vienna as a physician and neurologist. Later, he turned his attention to psychology and became the founder of psychoanalysis.

By the time of his death, 23 September 1939, in London, where he had sought asylum from the Nazi persecution of the Jews, his name was a landmark in 20th-century cultural history. In the words of the poet **W.H. Auden** (1907-73)…

if often he was wrong and, at times, absurd,
to us he is no more a person
now but a whole climate of opinion

under whom we conduct our different lives...

("In Memory of Sigmund Freud", 1939)

Contradictory Accusations

Freud's life and work have been subject to extraordinary investigation and attracted enduring, often contradictory, criticism.

HE HAS BEEN CHARGED WITH TELLING LIES ABOUT HIS CLINICAL PRACTICE, MORAL COWARDICE IN HIS THEORIZING, COLLUSION IN MEDICAL NEGLIGENCE AND OVERWEENING AMBITION.

... ACCUSED OF DRUG ADDICTION AND THE DEMONIZATION OF CHILDREN.

... REPROACHED FOR BOTH UNORIGINALITY AND MYTH-MAKING, STATING THE OBVIOUS AND MYSTIFYING US WITH THE OBSCURE.

BANG!

BOOM

BANG!

... HELD RESPONSIBLE FOR DELAYING OUR RECOGNITION OF INFANTILE SEXUAL ABUSE AND FOR THE INVENTION OF FALSE MEMORIES OF INFANTILE SEXUAL ABUSE.

... TO HAVE ENCOURAGED BOTH LIBERTINISM AND PURITANISM, MISOGYNY AND HOMOPHOBIA.

... HARBOURED INCESTUOUS CURIOSITY ABOUT HIS DAUGHTER, TO HAVE COMMITTED ADULTERY WITH HIS SISTER-IN-LAW AND TO HAVE PLANNED THE MURDER OF HIS FORMER FRIEND, WILHELM FLIESS.

BANG!

BANG!

Freud has been described as "an evil genius" and "one of the world's great hypocrites". And if all this were not enough, his theories have been blamed for alienating us from ourselves and undermining the very values upon which the whole of Western civilization is based.

The Death of Psychoanalysis

Opponents of psychoanalysis have anticipated its impending death from the moment it was born. Alfred Hoche, Professor of Psychiatry at Freiburg, took that view in a 1910 paper read at Baden-Baden. "On observing this movement, one can take comfort from one thing, namely the certainty… that it will abate before long."

"… A PSYCHICAL EPIDEMIC IN THE ANNALS OF MEDICINE", SAYS HOCHE.

ECHOED BY BORIS SIDIS, A PSYCHOPATHOLOGIST IN AMERICA - THE "MAD EPIDEMIC OF FREUDISM WHICH TAKES US BACK TO THE MIDDLE AGES…"

Again, in 1910, at a Congress of Neurologists and Psychiatrists in Hamburg, Professor Wilhelm Weygandt pounded the table with his fist: "This is not a topic for discussion at a scientific meeting; it is a matter for the police!" In 1911, David Eder presented the first paper on psychoanalysis to a meeting of the British Medical Association: "A Case of Obsession and Hysteria Treated by the Freud Psychoanalytic Method"…

In 1925, psychoanalysis was once more dismissed by another American psychologist J. McKeen Cattell as "not so much a question of science as a matter of taste, Dr Freud being an artist who lives in the fairyland of dreams among the ogres of perverted sex". **Karl Kraus** (1874-1936), the Viennese satirist, summed up the hostility to psychoanalysis in his magazine *Die Fackel* (*The Torch*): "Psychoanalysis is that mental illness for which it regards itself as therapy." But he went further…

This extreme vilification of psychoanalysis in the early 1900s has been sustained to our day. Compare what Kraus said then with the definition of "psychoanalyst" in Professor Stuart Sutherland's *Macmillan Dictionary of Psychology* (1989)…

THEY PICK OUR DREAMS AS IF THEY WERE OUR POCKETS…

… A PERSON WHO TAKES MONEY FROM ANOTHER ON THE PRETENCE THAT IT IS FOR THE OTHER'S OWN GOOD.

Stuart Sutherland

More recently, the British philosopher Roger Scruton condemned Freud in a BBC radio broadcast of May 2001.

Psychoanalysis has grown beyond what can be solely identified with Freud and his writings. Modern psychoanalytic theory and practice have evolved out of a hundred years of clinical experience accumulated on a worldwide basis. But a politicized movement against it continues to grow. A group in Britain calling itself *Psychotherapists and Counsellors for Social Responsibility* was formed in 1995 to speak out against racist, sexist and homophobic practices in psychoanalysis.

In 1996, the *New York Times* reported the postponement of a major exhibition on Sigmund Freud by the Library of Congress following protests by scholars. Nevertheless, even its most dedicated detractors today, such as Richard Webster in *Why Freud Was Wrong: Sin, Science and Psychoanalysis* (1995), must concede that psychoanalysis "has every claim to be regarded as richer and more original than any other single intellectual tradition in the 20th century". We should recall what Freud himself said to his colleagues at the second Psycho-Analytical Congress in 1910…

The continuing "Freud Wars" have deflected attention from the serious questions posed by psychoanalysis. Let's begin by seeing what these are…

Did Freud Invent the Unconscious?

Freud did not invent the notion of unconscious mental processes. In 1896, when he coined the term "psycho-analysis", the unconscious mind was already a fashionable idea among many 19th-century poets and philosophers of the "Romantic School", such as **William Wordsworth** (1770-1850) in England and **J.W. von Goethe** (1749-1832) in Germany.

Freud gave the notion of unconscious mental processes a new twist by claiming that they could be usefully investigated and modified.

Freud saw the mind as subject to the "dynamic forces" of instincts, urges, feelings, emotions and ideas. These were transformed or **displaced** from one object to another as they moved across the boundary of consciousness. Such "displacements" help us to bear unpleasant truths.

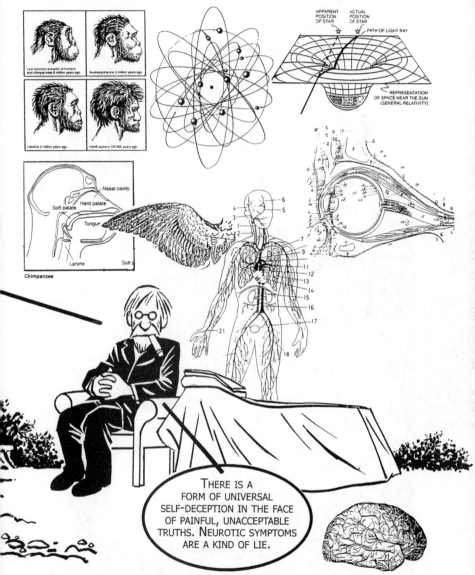

THERE IS A FORM OF UNIVERSAL SELF-DECEPTION IN THE FACE OF PAINFUL, UNACCEPTABLE TRUTHS. NEUROTIC SYMPTOMS ARE A KIND OF LIE.

In this way, Freud justified a new way of treating these symptoms – a way of helping people face the truth about themselves – based upon a prolonged and uniquely intimate dialogue between patient and doctor.

Strange Friendship

In 1887, a young ear, nose and throat specialist named **Wilhelm Fliess** (1858-1928) attended lectures given by Freud in Vienna. Fliess was about the same age as Freud and came from a similar background. Like Freud, he had a wide range of intellectual interests and both men were uninhibited by convention. They became firm friends.

FOR TEN YEARS, BETWEEN AUGUST 1890 AND SEPTEMBER 1900, WE CORRESPONDED REGULARLY.

WE ALSO MET FOR LONG WEEKEND "CONGRESSES" TO DISCUSS OUR IDEAS AND GIVE EACH OTHER MUTUAL SUPPORT.

Freud felt rejected by the medical establishment, but in his eyes Fliess was "the Kepler of biology" and his praise was "nectar and ambrosia".

Freud was then working on a general theory of psychology based on his notion of instinctual drive and its expression in psychic energy – to which he gave the name **libido**, from the Latin "lust" or "desire".

The Genital Nose

Freud marked the following passage in his copy of Fliess's 1902 book, *On the Causal Connection Between the Nose and the Sexual Organ*:

WOMEN WHO MASTURBATE ARE GENERALLY DYSMENORRHOEAL [HAVING PAINFUL OR DIFFICULT MENSTRUATION].

THEY CAN ONLY BE FINALLY CURED THROUGH AN OPERATION ON THE NOSE IF THEY TRULY GIVE UP THIS BAD PRACTICE.

Freud was so taken by Fliess's cranky ideas that he allowed him to operate twice on his own nose and called on him regularly to advise on the benefits of nasal surgery for his patients.

The Case of Emma Eckstein

Emma Eckstein was one of Freud's earliest analytic patients. She was 27 and, among other complaints, suffered from stomach ailments and menstrual problems. As the Freud critic Jeffrey Masson says in his 1984 book, *The Assault on Truth*, these complaints would undoubtedly have been attributed by both Freud and Fliess to masturbation. And probably Emma herself concurred in this view. Freud, and at his instigation Emma, underwent surgery with Fliess in early 1895. Freud was pleased with the results of his own operation.

I HAVE FELT QUITE UNBELIEVABLY WELL, AS THOUGH EVERYTHING HAD BEEN ERASED – A FEELING WHICH IN SPITE OF BETTER TIMES I HAVE NOT KNOWN FOR TEN MONTHS.

A Surgical Botch

But Emma's operation went badly wrong. She developed a severe post-operative infection accompanied by haemorrhages difficult to control.

EVENTUALLY, I CALLED IN ANOTHER SURGEON, IGNAZ ROSANES...

I REMOVED A PIECE OF IODOFORM GAUZE - AT LEAST HALF A METRE LONG - WHICH FLIESS HAD LEFT IN EMMA'S NOSE.

At this point, Emma had another severe haemorrhage, turned white and became pulseless.

Rosanes managed to control the bleeding quickly by repacking her nose with fresh gauze. Freud felt so sick that he was unable to remain in the room. Throughout these happenings, Emma had remained conscious.

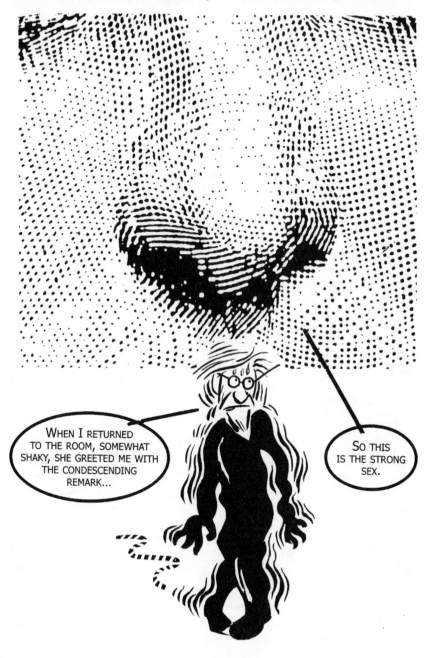

Bleeding From Hysteria

Emma's post-operative complications persisted for some time, to the evident frustration of her doctors, but she went on to make a full recovery and does not seem to have held the episode against either Freud or Fliess. In fact, she became a colleague of Freud and took on patients of her own for psychoanalytic treatment. But Masson, in his book, makes much of Freud's reaction, especially his unwillingness to ascribe blame to his friend and his overwillingness to blame the patient herself!

Despite the obvious reasons for Emma's post-operative condition, Freud preferred to attribute it, or most of it, to hysteria.

In May 1896, he wrote to Fliess: ... *so far as I know she bled out of* **longing**. *She has always been a bleeder, when cutting herself and in similar circumstances; as a child she suffered from severe nosebleeds; during the years when she was not yet menstruating, she had headaches which were interpreted to her as malingering and which in truth had been generated by suggestion... in the sanatorium, she became restless during the night because of an unconscious wish to entice me to go there...*

Did Freud Attempt Murder?

Freud's infatuation with Fliess finally came to an end in the summer of 1900, when they met for a holiday in the Austrian Tyrol by a lake called Achensee. According to Fliess, Freud took exception when he remarked that periodic biological processes were at work in the psyche…

Six years later, in a published account of the quarrel, he said Freud had shown "a violence towards me which was at first unintelligible to me". But in private Fliess told an even darker story to his daughter.

There is nothing to corroborate this story. Nor does it imply any manifest action on Freud's part. Freud later commented that Fliess had "developed a dreadful case of paranoia after throwing off his affection for me". Nonetheless, some commentators still go on thinking that Fliess had good reason to fear Freud's anger.

Was Freud a Drug Addict?

In 1884, cocaine was a little-known drug. Freud first read about its medical use in an obscure paper published by a German army doctor who had administered it to soldiers to improve their performance. Freud tried some himself and was impressed by the results. He found it lifted his depressions.

I THOUGHT I'D DISCOVERED AN EXTRAORDINARY PANACEA FOR MANY ILLS, AND GAVE IT TO MY FIANCÉE, MARTHA BERNAYS.

"WOE TO YOU MY PRINCESS, WHEN I COME, I WILL KISS YOU QUITE RED AND FEED YOU TIL' YOU ARE PLUMP. AND IF YOU ARE FORWARD YOU SHALL SEE WHO IS THE STRONGER A GENTLE LITTLE GIRL WHO DOESN'T EAT ENOUGH OR A BIG WILD MAN **WHO HAS COCAINE IN HIS BODY.**"

HE WENT OVERBOARD ON ITS VIRTUES.

Freud introduced cocaine to his friend, the physiologist **Ernst von Fleischl-Marxow** (1846-91), in the hope that it would cure his morphine addiction. It didn't. After an initial improvement, Fleischl-Marxow became much worse.

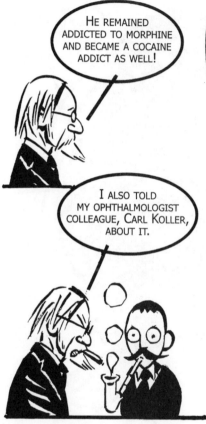

HE REMAINED ADDICTED TO MORPHINE AND BECAME A COCAINE ADDICT AS WELL!

I ALSO TOLD MY OPHTHALMOLOGIST COLLEAGUE, CARL KOLLER, ABOUT IT.

Freud published a paper advocating the use of cocaine for a variety of medical conditions. But the only useful application turned out to be as an anaesthetic for eye operations – for which, to Freud's chagrin, Koller took the credit. There is little reason to think that Freud himself was addicted to cocaine.

The Heavy Smoker

But Freud was addicted to tobacco. He found that he couldn't work without it. In 1895, he wrote to his friend Wilhelm Fliess about his inability to give up smoking. *"I began it again because I constantly missed it (after fourteen months abstinence) and because I must treat this psychic fellow well or he won't work for me. I demand a great deal of him."*

THE TORMENT, MOST OF THE TIME, IS SUPERHUMAN.

Freud paid a high price for his addiction, developing cancer of the jaw at the age of 67. He endured many operations and eventually had a large part of his lower jaw removed. He lived the next 15 years of his life in pain which became unbearable. Finally, he begged his doctor to put him out of his misery.

Problems with the Libido Theory

Freud's theory of the "libido" – his idea that the instincts could somehow be expressed in terms of "psychic energy" – was never operationally defined and therefore could not be measured.

The Conflict with Jung

Even within the psychoanalytic movement, Freud's bio-genetic libido theory aroused much dissent. Disagreement over the nature of libido was a major factor in Freud's conflict and eventual break with **Carl Gustav Jung** (1875-1961) – his favoured "crown prince of the movement".

We should take note here of Freud's "dualism" – a view that something must conflict with something else to produce psychological symptoms.

In 1912, Jung gave a successful series of lectures at the Jesuit University of Fordham in New York in which he presented his modifications of the Freudian theory of libido. He hoped that Freud would come to accept his views…

Jung went on to found his own school of "Analytic Psychology" after he broke off with Freud in 1913. Many psychoanalysts have since jettisoned the whole libido theory. However, we will see now why Freud always insisted on a "dualism" – a conflict of two fundamentally opposing forces in psychic life.

Is There a Death Instinct?

In 1920, Freud proposed a new and even more controversial theory of the *death instinct*. Till then, Freud had accepted an opposition between **sexual instincts** (represented by love) which focus on another person or object for their satisfaction and **self-preservative instincts** (such as hunger). He now saw that aggression and destruction arise neither as responses to the need for self-preservation nor as components of sexual desire.

THERE IS A COMPLETELY SEPARATE INSTINCTUAL TENDENCY – THE DEATH INSTINCT – AND THIS TOO IS GROUNDED IN BIOLOGICAL ACTIVITY.

Freud perceived an instinct that lies "beyond the pleasure principle". What does he mean? He asks: why do humans so often repeat painful experiences? Masochism is an obvious example. Freud at first saw this as a "secondary process" – a turning inwards of outwardly directed aggression. But then he wondered if there might be a "primary masochism" as a product of the death instinct.

Murderers who kill themselves, as often happens, might suggest that this is true. But such extreme instances of suicide and sadomasochism are rare and insufficient to generate a theory.

The Anxiety of Play

Freud also found evidence of the normal tendency to manufacture stress in an unexpected source. He watched his grandson repeatedly throw a treasured toy away. Why should he subject himself to this loss? Then he saw him throw a cotton reel on a piece of string over the side of his cot and pull it back.

I WAS STRUCK BY THE GAME AS A RE-ENACTMENT OF PAINFUL SEPARATIONS - WEANING AND THE LOSS OF MATERNAL CLOSENESS.

Although the recovery of the wooden reel was an occasion for joy, why, Freud asks, should the initial act of throwing away (often repeated as a game in its own right) produce such satisfaction?

This method of coping with neediness, by killing it off rather than joining the struggle to find a need-satisfying object, can lead to severe neurotic restriction if it becomes a dominant character trait in later life.

Our Own Worst Enemies

Psychoanalytic practice also convinced Freud that patients compulsively repeat emotionally painful situations. He found them re-enacting disappointments which could be traced back to unpleasant experiences in childhood. And why should patients have negative therapeutic reactions and undermine their own progress? Besides, there are people with no apparent neurosis who seem to repeat the same emotional mistakes over and over again...

Perhaps not surprisingly, Freud's idea of a death instinct came to him shortly after the frightful carnage of the First World War, 1914-18. He had the evidence of battle-shock neuroses and post-traumatic stresses which were characterized by "flashbacks" and compulsive reliving of the painful traumas in nightmares.

IF DREAMS ARE CONSTRUCTED ON THE PRINCIPLE OF **WISH-FULFILMENT,** WHY SHOULD THESE UNPLEASANT EXPERIENCES RECUR?

Is the nightmare a kind of warning device, a vehicle for pre-empting further trauma – an attempt to **mobilize anxiety** in order to ensure that defences remain in place against future stresses?

Life in Co-operation with Death

Freud pulls all these threads together to weave an extravagant and sweeping psycho-biological myth. There exists in all living things a built-in drive towards disintegration, an innate tendency to return to less complicated forms and to decompose. Each organism is programmed to die **in its own time**…

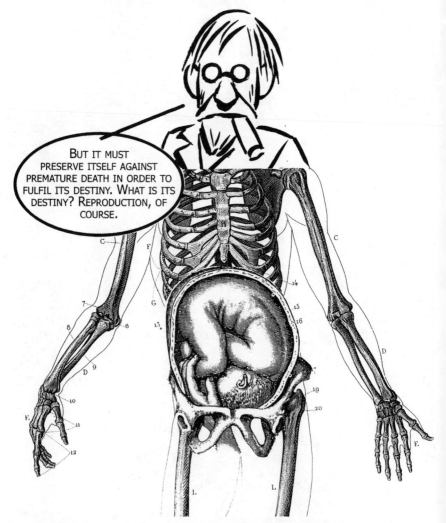

BUT IT MUST PRESERVE ITSELF AGAINST PREMATURE DEATH IN ORDER TO FULFIL ITS DESTINY. WHAT IS ITS DESTINY? REPRODUCTION, OF COURSE.

The death drive is countered ultimately by the need to bring male and female germ cells together. This is the basis for creativity, integration and the development of more complex forms – a life drive, to which Freud gives the name **Eros**.

The psychoanalyst Erich Fromm points out that whereas the pleasure principle had portrayed man as primarily egotistical, Freud's new Eros theory is entirely different. Man is no longer conceived as a kind of isolated pleasure-seeking machine, but impelled by his life instinct to seek union with others.

LIFE, LOVE AND GROWTH ARE ONE AND THE SAME, MORE DEEPLY ROOTED AND FUNDAMENTAL THAN SEXUALITY AND MERE PLEASURE.

IF I AM ASKED - "AM I MYSELF CONVINCED OF THE TRUTH OF THESE HYPOTHESES?" - I WOULD ANSWER THAT I AM NOT AND DO NOT SEEK TO PERSUADE OTHERS TO BELIEVE IN THEM.

Beyond the Pleasure Principle is a fascinating book, ingeniously argued, but in which Freud admits his uncertainty.

Is it True Biology?

Despite Freud's uncertainty, is he so far from the modern neo-Darwinist conception of "the selfish gene"? If our evolutionary function is to "carry and disperse" our DNA, our bodies need only function well enough to accomplish this purpose. Life after reproduction and child-rearing would be an abnormal bonus.

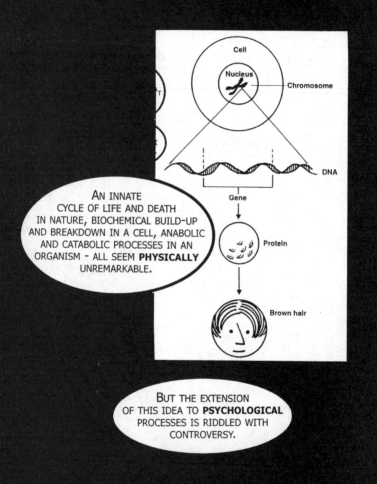

AN INNATE CYCLE OF LIFE AND DEATH IN NATURE, BIOCHEMICAL BUILD-UP AND BREAKDOWN IN A CELL, ANABOLIC AND CATABOLIC PROCESSES IN AN ORGANISM - ALL SEEM **PHYSICALLY** UNREMARKABLE.

BUT THE EXTENSION OF THIS IDEA TO **PSYCHOLOGICAL** PROCESSES IS RIDDLED WITH CONTROVERSY.

Freud's attempt to base his new instinct theory in biology not only failed to find a credible somatic source for the death instinct, but denied his own conceptual progress.

Freud's Idea of Aggression

In Freud's view of the death instinct's manifestations, aggression and destructiveness are used more or less synonymously. There can be no aggression without destructiveness (though it may be mitigated by fusion with constructive forces).

THE DEATH INSTINCT, WHICH IS CLINICALLY "SILENT", MAKES ITSELF KNOWN MAINLY AFTER ITS DIRECTION HAS BEEN **ALTERED** SO THAT IT POINTS OUTWARDS IN THE FORM OF ATTACKS ON OTHERS.

Most important, the instinct is "gratuitous", i.e. motiveless, given by the body's ineluctable progression towards death, and is not brought into being by external provocation or frustration.

Criticism of Freud's Views

Freud's propositions on aggression are questionable. The psychoanalyst Henri Parens, in a rigorous observational study of the development of aggression in early childhood, distinguished four different types.

WITHIN HOURS OF BIRTH, YOU CAN DISCERN DESTRUCTIVE BEHAVIOUR LINKED TO PHYSICAL DISCOMFORT...

... AS WELL AS SO-CALLED NON-AFFECTIVE DESTRUCTIVENESS, I.E. NORMAL FEEDING AND SUCKING, THE BREAKDOWN OF FOOD BY DIGESTION, ETC.

But he also found **non-destructive** aggression during the first three months of life, characterized by exploratory behaviour aimed at mastery, and finally **pleasure-related** destructiveness which seemed to be a late development towards the end of the first year of life.

Not only are aggression and destructiveness capable of being separated but also it is questionable whether either can be equated with the body's progress towards its natural expiry date. Once again, as Erich Fromm puts it: *"If we assume, following Freud's reasoning on the basis of the repetition compulsion, that life has an inherent tendency for slowing down and eventually to die, such a biological innate tendency would be quite different from the active impulse to destroy. If we add that this same tendency to die is also supposed to be the source of the passion for power and the instinct for mastery, and – when mixed with sexuality – the source of sadism and masochism, the theoretical **tour de force** must end in failure."*

Freud's theory of a death instinct is scientifically flawed, but, as he himself admitted, it was a speculation. Many critics have mobilized this speculative side of Freud to disprove or discredit **everything** he said. Let's consider a famous example, the "Anna O" case...

A Diagnosis of Hysteria

The "Anna O" case is important in the prehistory of psychoanalysis because this young woman's illness was recorded by Freud and **Josef Breuer** (1842-1925) in their *Studies of Hysteria* (1895).

... THROUGH REGULAR DIALOGUES WITH ME, CARRIED OUT WHILE SHE WAS UNDER HYPNOSIS.

I INVENTED THE TERM "TALKING CURE" TO DESCRIBE THE PROCESS BY WHICH I GAINED TEMPORARY RELIEF FROM MY MANY SYMPTOMS...

IT IS HYSTERIA – AN ILLNESS INCONSISTENT WITH ANY KNOWN OR IDENTIFIABLE **PHYSICAL** DISORDER.

Some critics have questioned this diagnosis of hysteria. But the experimental psychologist **H.J. Eysenck** (1916-1997) in his book, *The Decline and Fall of the Freudian Empire* (1985), hurries over-eagerly to disprove Freud. Eysenck is not a physician, and although distanced from the events by a hundred years, he has no doubt of his own diagnosis…

In fact, Eysenck's "diagnosis" was first promulgated by the historian E.M. Thornton. But is it correct? Lack of medical knowledge led them both to commit a "howler". Untreated tuberculous meningitis is fatal within 6 to 8 weeks, but Anna O, whose real name was Bertha Pappenheim, went on to become a well-known social worker and feminist.

Anything But Hysteria

Eysenck's selective use of evidence and anti-psychoanalytical bias undermine his claim to scientific objectivity. Equally unconvincing is Richard Webster's argument in *Why Freud Was Wrong*. He acknowledges that Anna O could not have been suffering from tuberculous meningitis.

BUT I ALIGN MYSELF WITH THOSE WHO THINK THAT HYSTERIA IS AND WAS A NON-EXISTENT CONDITION – AN ARBITRARY LABEL TO COVER MEDICAL IGNORANCE...

HE THEREFORE PROPOSES THAT **ALL** THE PATIENTS DESCRIBED BY BREUER AND ME, WERE SUFFERING FROM YET OTHER "UNDIAGNOSED DISEASES".

Lateral fissure

A well-known adage informing the diagnostic practice of doctors states that "common conditions occur commonly", but this does not appear to have percolated into Webster's thinking. High on his list of differential diagnoses are the relatively unusual conditions of temporal lobe epilepsy and Gilles de la Tourette's syndrome.

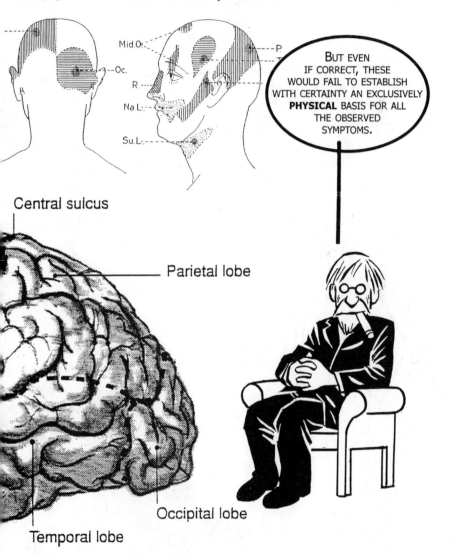

Central sulcus

BUT EVEN IF CORRECT, THESE WOULD FAIL TO ESTABLISH WITH CERTAINTY AN EXCLUSIVELY **PHYSICAL** BASIS FOR ALL THE OBSERVED SYMPTOMS.

Parietal lobe

Occipital lobe

Temporal lobe

In any event, it is obvious that contemporary psychoanalysis can neither be substantiated nor undermined by recourse to the dubious re-diagnosis of 19th-century cases.

What is Truthful Science?

Eysenck and other proclaimed scientific judges tend to a "double standard" in their use of evidence against psychoanalysis.

Eysenck, in particular, bolsters his argument against the efficacy of psychoanalytic treatment by making extravagant and unfounded claims for behavioural therapy.

In reality, every psychiatrist and clinical psychologist knows that obsessive-compulsive symptoms can be amongst the most intractable and do not always respond to behaviour therapy, drugs or electroconvulsive therapy. For this reason, sufferers form a significant proportion of those patients undergoing psycho-surgery.

Science or Religion?

The charge that psychoanalysis is a religion requiring the eye of faith rather than the observation of fact was levelled in 1910 by Alfred Hoche: *"… we are not dealing with facts capable of being tested or proved scientifically, but with articles of faith. In fact, if I exclude some of the more rational adherents, we are dealing with a congregation of believers, a kind of sect with all its characteristics."*

Jung echoed this in his 1913 American Lectures.

Many contemporary psychoanalysts who embrace an interpretative position think that symbols and "meanings" exist in a non-deterministic "linguistic" world, unconstrained by biological reality, unamenable to scientific investigation.

But Freud was uncompromising in his claims. In his famous 1932 Lecture entitled *The Question of a Weltanschauung*, he made it clear that he regarded psychoanalysis as a specialist science, a branch of psychology which systematically investigated the workings of the human mind by observation and inference in the same manner as other natural sciences. There was no place, he said, for intuition, revelation or divination.

*"It is not permissible to declare that science is one field of human mental activity and that religion and philosophy are others, at least its equal in value, and that science has no business to interfere with the other two: that they all have an equal claim to be true and that everyone is at liberty to choose from which he will draw his convictions and in which he will place his belief. A view of this kind is regarded as particularly superior, tolerant, broad-minded and free from illiberal prejudices. Unfortunately it is not tenable and shares all the pernicious features of an entirely unscientific **Weltanschauung** [universal world-view] and is equivalent to one in practice."*

IT IS SIMPLY A FACT THAT THE TRUTH CANNOT BE TOLERANT, THAT IT ADMITS OF NO COMPROMISES OR LIMITATIONS, THAT RESEARCH REGARDS EVERY SPHERE OF HUMAN ACTIVITY AS BELONGING TO IT AND THAT IT MUST BE RELENTLESSLY CRITICAL IF ANY OTHER POWER TRIES TO TAKE OVER ANY PART OF IT.

Scientific Empiricism, Realism, Determinism

SCIENTIFIC THEORIES MUST PRODUCE AN ACCOUNT WHICH ULTIMATELY CORRESPONDS WITH A CAUSALLY EXPLAINED OBSERVABLE REALITY. TO THE EXTENT THAT THEY ACCURATELY CARRY OUT THIS FUNCTION, THEY ARE TRUE.

MANY WHO SHARE FREUD'S **EMPIRICIST**, **REALIST** AND **DETERMINIST** VIEW OF SCIENCE DISAGREE THAT PSYCHOANALYSIS BELONGS IN THAT CATEGORY.

HIS PLACE IS NOT, AS HE CLAIMED, WITH COPERNICUS AND DARWIN, BUT WITH HANS CHRISTIAN ANDERSEN AND THE BROTHERS GRIMM, TELLERS OF FAIRY TALES.

FREUD IS A GENIUS, NOT OF SCIENCE, BUT OF PROPAGANDA, NOT OF RIGOROUS PROOF, BUT OF PERSUASION, NOT OF THE DESIGN OF EXPERIMENTS, BUT OF LITERARY ART.

It is surprising that after almost a century the issue remains hot. This is an important debate which involves consideration of both the nature of *science* – itself a **branch of philosophy** – and the extent to which psychoanalysis conforms to its canons. The difficulty remains in defining not only exactly what science is but also what psychoanalysis is and how we should think about it.

Fairy Tales and Scientific Theories

Fairy tales may perform important psychological functions. Like myth and scripture, they reconcile us to reality, providing a framework for making sense out of life, but they are essentially unchanging. Nothing that contradicts religious dogma can alter the basic story.

PRIESTS AND THEOLOGIANS WILL TRY TO PERSUADE US THAT **WE** ARE IN ERROR IF WE ARE NOT CONVINCED.

EITHER WE HAVE MISINTERPRETED THE STORY...

OR EVIDENCE WHICH APPEARS TO CONTRADICT THE STORY CAN BE BROUGHT INTO LINE THROUGH FAITH - GOD'S EXISTENCE IS ABSOLUTE, THE STORY NEED NOT BE CHANGED.

So, is Freudian psychoanalysis like this? Are psychoanalysts a coterie of believers capable of reconciling any observed evidence with their underlying belief in the unconscious mind?

Science bears a different relationship to empirical reality. Its stories (theories) are always provisional, always open to correction by new observations.

A THEORY WHICH CANNOT BE CORRECTED - CANNOT BE **DISCONFIRMED** BY EMPIRICAL OBSERVATIONS - IS NOT SCIENTIFIC.

THUS, ACCORDING TO THE PHILOSOPHER **KARL POPPER** (1902-94), A SCIENTIFIC THEORY MUST BE ABLE TO SPECIFY THE EMPIRICAL OBSERVATIONS THAT WOULD **FALSIFY** IT.

Can psychoanalysis do this? Can there be a scientific theory of meaning and of symbol formation? Let's examine these questions...

Symbol Formation

A symbol can be regarded as something in somebody's mind which stands for something else.

Features like these have been categorized by philologists in well-known figures of speech.

Similes explicitly liken one thing to another, as in Craig Raine's poem, *The Behaviour of Dogs...*

> *scratch their itches*
> *like one-legged cyclists sprinting*
> *for home*
>
> *pee like hurdlers,*
> *shit like weightlifters.*

Metaphors go one step further and omit the "as if" statement. In metonymy, something is represented by something else associated with it – boxing by "the ring" or psychoanalysis by "the couch". In synecdoche, a part represents the whole. Being "given one's head" expresses the larger concept of freedom, a "bit of skirt" can mean a woman, a "hunk" can be a sexually desirable man.

Arbitrary or Motivated?

A symbol may share nothing in common with what it represents. In fact, most words fall into this category and are linked to their referent purely by arbitrary convention, as are algebraic expressions. To distinguish this kind of "conventional" symbol from others, they are sometimes referred to as "signs". Symbols are often smaller, less complex and more concrete than the thing they symbolize. A flag may represent a nation, a pair of scales the abstract concept of justice. This is a big subject which concerns linguistics, philosophy, anthropology, art and religious history.

BUT IS THERE A COHERENT PSYCHOANALYTIC THEORY OF SYMBOLISM?

THE PROBLEM IS HOW TO IDENTIFY SYMBOLISM? IS IT PURELY ARBITRARY OR MOTIVATED BY DESIRES?

Freud's Theory of Symbolism

Freud did not discover sexual symbolism. It had existed in works of art and literature since the dawn of cultural history. But he directed attention to the way it could be manufactured in the unconscious mind, and more controversially, insisted on its universal occurrence. Freud came to recognize that certain elements of symbolism in dreams cannot be explained in terms only of an individual's personal history but are held in common by the whole of mankind.

THESE ARE DEEP BASIC ELEMENTS THAT CONCERN BIRTH, SEX, DEATH... AND MUST BE INTERPRETED FROM THE ANALYST'S OWN KNOWLEDGE OF CULTURE, FOLKLORE, RELIGION, ART, ETC.

A Universal Pool of Symbols

Freud lists some of these commonly used sexual symbols…

Children in dreams often stand for the genitals; and, indeed, both men and women are in the habit of referring to their genitals affectionately as "their little ones". Stekel is right in recognizing a "little brother" as the penis. Playing with a little child, beating it, etc., often represents masturbation in dreams. To represent castration symbolically, the dream-work makes use of baldness, hair-cutting, falling out of teeth

and decapitation. *If one of the ordinary symbols for a penis occurs in a dream doubled or multiplied, it is to be regarded as a warding-off of castration. The appearance in dreams of lizards – animals whose tails grow again if they are pulled off – has the same significance. Many of the beasts which are used as genital symbols in mythology and folk-lore play the same part in dreams: e.g. fishes, snails, cats, mice (on account of the pubic hair), and above all those most important symbols of the male organ – snakes. Small animals and vermin represent small children – for instance undesired brothers and sisters. Being plagued with vermin is often a sign of pregnancy.*

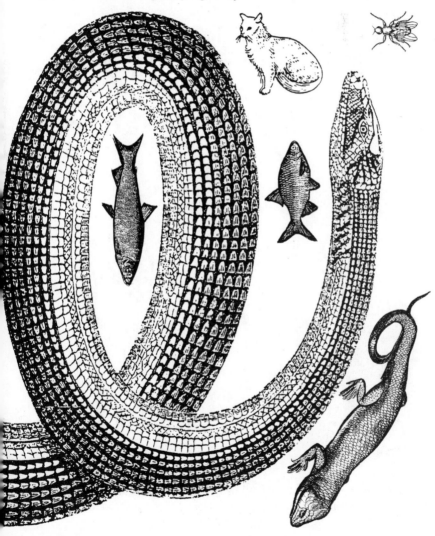

An Unscientific Theory of Symbolism

Freud believed that such universal symbols could be traced back to their origin in the evolutionary history of the human species. He adopted the mistaken evolutionary theory of **J.-B. de Monet Lamarck** (1744-1829) which proposed the notion of "acquired characteristics".

> CHANGES TO AN ORGANISM'S BODY, DUE TO HABITS FORMED IN ITS LIFETIME, CAN BE **INHERITED** BY THAT INDIVIDUAL'S OFFSPRING.

> SO, ALSO, MENTAL CHARACTERISTICS - SUCH AS MEMORIES ACQUIRED DURING AN ORGANISM'S LIFETIME - CAN BE **BIOLOGICALLY** TRANSMITTED DOWN THE GENERATIONS.

Freud's account is fatally flawed by this "psycho-Lamarckism". Is there anything in Freud's interpretation of dreams that can be scientifically defended?

Dream Interpretation

Freud pioneered a revolutionary new interpretative method of **free association**. He had experimented earlier with various unsatisfactory techniques – hypnosis, suggestion, even massaging the patient's head. Free association means that I "let go" of my normal self-critical reflection and follow thoughts wherever they might lead. This provides the analyst with observational data from which unconscious desires could be inferred.

THE UNCONSCIOUS ROOTS OF SYMPTOMS, DREAMS AND DESIRES ARE REVEALED BY FREE ASSOCIATION...

IT IS THE KEY TO UNDOING **REPRESSION**.

But if I say "whatever comes into my mind", can this prove that what emerges is in fact organized by some unconscious principle? Is it a real property of the unconscious mind? Or is it imposed by some other "observing agency"? This is a real problem for Freudianism.

Wish-Fulfilment in Dreams

A dream-world is not simply an hallucinated version of waking reality. It may have a "real" substance and yet allow all sorts of impossible happenings. A single person may be uncannily more than one. A place may be several places. Time may run backwards...

DREAMS LIBERATE US FROM THE NORMAL CONSTRAINTS OF REALITY AND THUS FROM THE NEED TO AVOID **CONFLICT** BY SUPPRESSING INSTINCTUAL CRAVINGS.

DREAMS CAN GENERATE EXPERIENCES THAT NOT ONLY FULFIL REALISTIC DESIRES BUT ALSO WISHES UNATTAINABLE IN EVERYDAY LIFE.

A student in a cold bedroom may dream that her radiator is on – but also that she's once again an infant at her mother's breast.

Although dreams allow expression of material normally unacceptable to the conscious mind, Freud thought the ban was only partially lifted. That the offending impulses were encoded to cheat the "censor" before reaching awareness. Dreams, like hysterical symptoms, could be seen as **compromise formations** – disguised manifestations of unconscious conflict. Self-analysis of his own dreams forced him towards uncongenial conclusions about himself.

ALL DREAMS ARE "WOLVES IN SHEEP'S CLOTHING" - NONE ARE GUILELESS, ALL SHOW "THE MARK OF THE BEAST".

Let's look at one of his famous specimen dreams, "Irma's Injection"…

Irma's Injection: Recorded 23/24 July 1895

A LARGE HALL - NUMEROUS GUESTS, WHOM WE WERE RECEIVING. - AMONG THEM WAS IRMA. I AT ONCE TOOK HER ON ONE SIDE, AS THOUGH TO ANSWER HER LETTER AND TO REPROACH HER FOR NOT HAVING ACCEPTED MY "SOLUTION" YET.

I WAS ALARMED AND LOOKED AT HER. SHE LOOKED PALE AND PUFFY. I THOUGHT TO MYSELF THAT AFTER ALL I MUST BE MISSING SOME ORGANIC TROUBLE. I TOOK HER TO THE WINDOW AND LOOKED DOWN HER THROAT, AND SHE SHOWED SIGNS OF RECALCITRANCE...

SHE THEN OPENED HER MOUTH PROPERLY AND ON THE RIGHT I FOUND A BIG WHITE PATCH; AT ANOTHER PLACE I SAW EXTENSIVE WHITISH GREY SCABS UPON SOME REMARKABLE CURLY STRUCTURES WHICH WERE EVIDENTLY MODELLED ON THE TURBINAL BONES OF THE NOSE. - I AT ONCE CALLED IN DR. M., AND HE REPEATED THE EXAMINATION AND CONFIRMED IT...

DR. M. LOOKED QUITE DIFFERENT FROM USUAL; HE WAS VERY PALE, HE WALKED WITH A LIMP AND HIS CHIN WAS CLEAN-SHAVEN...

MY FRIEND OTTO WAS NOW STANDING BESIDE HER AS WELL, AND MY FRIEND LEOPOLD WAS PERCUSSING HER THROUGH HER BODICE...

SHE HAS A DULL AREA LOW DOWN ON THE LEFT.

HE ALSO INDICATED THAT A PORTION OF THE SKIN ON THE LEFT SHOULDER WAS INFILTRATED. (I NOTICED THIS, JUST AS HE DID, IN SPITE OF HER DRESS.)

WE WERE DIRECTLY AWARE, TOO, OF THE ORIGIN OF THE INFECTION. NOT LONG BEFORE, WHEN SHE WAS FEELING UNWELL, MY FRIEND OTTO HAD GIVEN HER AN INJECTION OF A PREPARATION OF PROPYL, PROPYLS... PROPRIONIC ACID... TRIMETHYLAMIN (AND I SAW BEFORE ME THE FORMULA FOR THIS PRINTED IN HEAVY TYPE)...

(FREUD, THE INTERPRETATION OF DREAMS (1900), P. 107)

During the summer of 1895, Freud had been giving treatment to a young lady, Anna Hammarschlag, who was a friend of the family. She was the daughter of his old Bible teacher. He was also treating Emma Eckstein then, but the Irma in his dream is now thought to have been Anna. Freud was concerned that any failure in treatment would threaten his old established friendship with the family. In fact, the treatment ended with only "partial success". The patient was less anxious but had not lost all her somatic symptoms. Freud proposed some course of action, which he does not specify, and Anna (Irma) broke off the treatment.

LATER THAT YEAR, I HAD A VISIT FROM A JUNIOR COLLEAGUE - OTTO - WHO HAD BEEN STAYING WITH MY PATIENT...

SHE'S BETTER BUT NOT QUITE WELL.

I FELT ANNOYED BY THIS REPROOF BUT I SHOWED NO OUTWARD SIGN OF MY FEELING.

Indeed, he says it did not really become clear to him until he analysed the dream which he had on the following morning.

Sexual Undertones

This is the first dream that Freud submits to illustrate his method of working. It is triggered (in line with his theory) by material from the preceding day, yet although the dream seems to fulfil one of Freud's unconscious wishes, it is not a sexual one deriving from infancy, as his theory demanded, but rather an only mildly unacceptable "adult" wish.

References to Irma's "bodice" and her skin seen "in spite of her dress" are sexually indicative. What does Freud make of these hints?

"We naturally used to examine the children in the hospital undressed: and this would be a contrast to the manner in which adult female patients have to be examined. I remembered that it was said of a celebrated clinician that he never made a physical examination of his patients except through their clothes. Further than this I could not see. Frankly, I had no desire to penetrate more deeply at this point."

Freud seems deliberately to tease us with an unveiled hint. The philosopher **Ludwig Wittgenstein** (1889-1951) commented shrewdly on this scruple.

FREUD VERY COMMONLY GIVES WHAT WE MIGHT CALL A SEXUAL INTERPRETATION.

BUT IT IS INTERESTING THAT AMONG ALL THE REPORTS OF DREAMS WHICH HE GIVES, THERE IS NOT A SINGLE EXAMPLE OF A STRAIGHTFORWARD SEXUAL DREAM. YET THESE ARE AS COMMON AS RAIN.

Truth or Self-Deception?

Freud concentrates on his unconscious wish to blame his friends for the bad medical outcome. To get a second opinion, he calls in a colleague, Dr. M., who "looked quite different from usual; he was very pale, he walked with a limp and his chin was clean-shaven…".

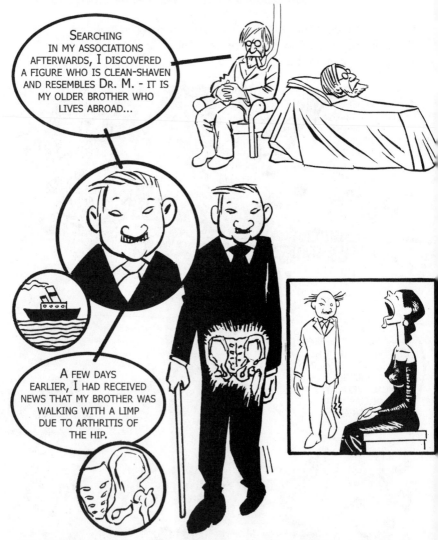

SEARCHING IN MY ASSOCIATIONS AFTERWARDS, I DISCOVERED A FIGURE WHO IS CLEAN-SHAVEN AND RESEMBLES DR. M. - IT IS MY OLDER BROTHER WHO LIVES ABROAD…

A FEW DAYS EARLIER, I HAD RECEIVED NEWS THAT MY BROTHER WAS WALKING WITH A LIMP DUE TO ARTHRITIS OF THE HIP.

This leads to a further link – both Dr. M. and his brother had rejected a certain suggestion, and he was in an ill-humour with them. Can we take it that free association has revealed the dream image to be a fusion of those two figures?

Freud's dream apparently constructs a scenario in which his professional reputation is vindicated from charges of negligence. If so, it is hardly a "disguised wish". Far from always being misleading disguises for "bestial" wishes, dreams are often vehicles for truth-telling. Direct access occurs to preoccupations of which we were hitherto unaware.

DREAMS **DO** DISGUISE...

YES, BUT THEY DO OTHER THINGS TOO!

Freud over-emphasizes self-deception and tends to generalize unduly. Dreams are far richer than his restricted theory of disguised wish-fulfilment allows. But his free-associative method of interpretation has succeeded nevertheless to reveal more meaning than his theory grants.

A Scientific Theory of Symbolism

The process of free association can serve to "unpack" certain symbols that are specific to events in a particular dreamer's life and cannot be understood without recourse to intimate personal history. These symbols are created by "dream-work", which transforms latent thoughts – unconscious representations of desire – into manifest dreams.

I DO NOT REGARD THESE AS "TRUE" SYMBOLS BUT AS DISGUISES FOR UNACCEPTABLE WISHES.

WHAT IS DISGUISED CAN BECOME KNOWN BY **REVERSING** THE DREAM-WORK THROUGH FREE ASSOCIATION.

What is unacceptable to us can be repressed or disguised by defences against it. If we agree on that likely fact, then we can discern a psychological theory which meets the requirements of a logical science based on empirical observation.

Such diverse phenomena as hysterical symptoms, slips of the tongue, bungled actions, distorted memories and the contents of dreams can reasonably be brought together, as Freud did, and understood as defensive products. The theory suggests that, far from being a language, these symbolic occurrences are a kind of *anti*-language or *motivated* mistake.

THEY BELONG IN AN INDIVIDUAL'S OWN DEVELOPMENTAL HISTORY AND ARE A FORM OF SELF-DECEPTION BY WHICH INDIVIDUAL DESIRE CAN BE MISREPRESENTED TO OURSELVES.

This does not occur in any arbitrary way. It is not dictated by the conventions of language. Rather, the process is determined by the nature of empirical reality and the way we experience it. Individual repression, as conveyed by our own symbolic productions, is therefore capable of being investigated by science.

Objections to "Dream Meaning"

Yet should we regard what emerges from a web of free associations as "the meaning of a dream"? Or would the same web have been generated from any point of departure? Do the contents of a dream really give us privileged access to the unconscious mind? Wittgenstein objected that they do not.

WHENEVER YOU ARE PREOCCUPIED WITH SOMETHING, WITH SOME TROUBLE OR WITH SOME PROBLEM WHICH IS A BIG THING IN YOUR LIFE - AS SEX IS FOR INSTANCE...

... THEN NO MATTER WHERE YOU **START FROM,** THE ASSOCIATION WILL LEAD FINALLY AND INEVITABLY BACK TO THAT **SAME THEME.**

FREUD REMARKS ON HOW, AFTER THE ANALYSIS OF IT, THE DREAM APPEARS VERY LOGICAL. AND OF COURSE IT DOES.

YOU COULD START WITH ANY OF THE OBJECTS ON THIS TABLE – WHICH CERTAINLY ARE NOT PUT THERE THROUGH YOUR DREAM ACTIVITY – AND YOU COULD FIND THAT THEY ALL COULD BE CONNECTED IN A PATTERN LIKE THAT...

AND THE PATTERN WOULD BE LOGICAL IN THE SAME WAY.

Note that Wittgenstein concurs in thinking that a chain of free-associations will inevitably lead back to "a big thing". Psychoanalysts would find little to argue with here. But the notion that all associative roads lead eventually to Rome does not prevent the "Royal Road" of dream from being better trodden. Since the content of a dream originates in a person's own imagination, is it not also likely to be related to "a big thing"? And if so, provide a better spring-board to self-knowledge than some random object?

Identifying the Dream-Work

Freud identifies several key mechanisms that operate in dream-work –
condensation, **displacement** and **symbolization**. Briefly, how do
these function?

Condensation means that one simple image or memory in a dream can
stand for several unrelated or contradictory wishes.

Displacement separates an emotional charge from its real object and
attaches it to an entirely different one.

Symbolization is visual imagery that distorts or disguises the expression of sexual objects and relations to evade repression.

Is Meaning Imposed on Dream?

What is the force of this sceptical argument? Consider the construction of a known symbolic entity – the Union Jack. The red cross of St George was first superimposed upon the white cross of St Andrew, and about 200 years later the cross of St Patrick was added when Ireland was legally united with Great Britain in 1801. The three flags were thus "condensed" into a single emblem of national unity.

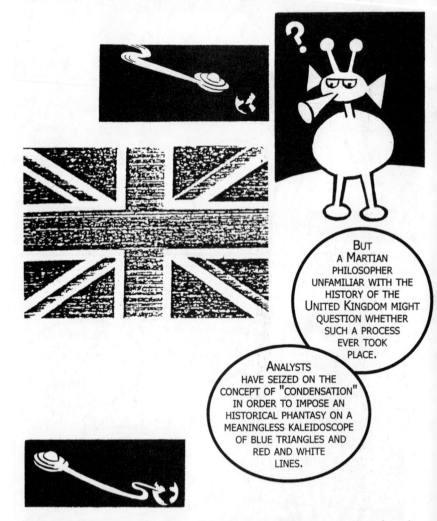

BUT A MARTIAN PHILOSOPHER UNFAMILIAR WITH THE HISTORY OF THE UNITED KINGDOM MIGHT QUESTION WHETHER SUCH A PROCESS EVER TOOK PLACE.

ANALYSTS HAVE SEIZED ON THE CONCEPT OF "CONDENSATION" IN ORDER TO IMPOSE AN HISTORICAL PHANTASY ON A MEANINGLESS KALEIDOSCOPE OF BLUE TRIANGLES AND RED AND WHITE LINES.

Indeed, but if extant examples of the component flags were then found – if the Grand Union flag of 1606 was discovered – then the circumstantial evidence against the sceptical philosopher would be strong.

Clinical experience regularly confirms the value of associations to dream material in enlarging a person's self-awareness. In the psychoanalytical situation, dreams that start by being opaque to the dreamer and emotionally neutral frequently generate ideas, memories and feelings that can help a person to know what he thinks and to understand hitherto bewildering states of mind.

What is "Transference Love"?

On the very evening when Breuer thought he had cured Anna O of all her hysteria symptoms, he was called back in an emergency to find her confused and writhing with abdominal cramps.

Breuer fled the house in a "cold sweat". He lost the opportunity to deal with Anna's "love" fantasies. Freud, on the other hand, threw professional caution to the wind and came to welcome such experiences as a process for which he coined the term *transference*.

...erence is a concept central to the modern theory of ...oanalytic knowledge. Clearly, if transference does not guara... ...le insights into a patient's inner world, then the rationale for t... ... therapeutic procedure is severely undermined.

...s Dora case history is certainly no proof that transference ex... ...o answer to sceptical disbelief, nor does he offer it as one; bu... ...es us to understand what transference might be if we happe...

The Dora Case

In October 1900, Freud commenced the treatment of a young woman, "Dora", suffering from a range of troublesome symptoms. In addition to a history of nervous cough and loss of voice, she was depressed and dissatisfied with herself and out of sorts with her parents.

However, when her parents found a suicide note in her writing desk, she reluctantly acquiesced in a referral to Freud.

Dora's father, a successful businessman, suffered from both chronic granulomas common at the turn of the century – tuberculosis and syphilis. He had been nursed in his illness by a close friend of the family, Frau K.

HE HAD HOPED FOR MY SUPPORT IN TALKING DORA OUT OF THE CONVICTION THAT HE WAS HAVING A LONG-TERM AFFAIR WITH FRAU K...

I'M CONVINCED THAT HER SYMPTOMS ARE RELATED TO THE PERSISTENT PRESSURE SHE EXERTS ON ME TO BREAK OFF RELATIONS WITH THE K FAMILY.

KOF! KOF!

In addition, Dora alleged that Herr K, a man in his forties, had propositioned her on two occasions, once when she was 14 years old and again, two years later, when she was spending a summer holiday with the K's by a lake in the Alps.

Dora Sees Clearly...

Dora's father chose to believe Herr K's version of the story which attributed the whole thing to the girl's imagination.

BUT HE WAS INSINCERE IN APPEALING TO ME TO BRING HIS DAUGHTER "TO REASON"... HE KNEW THAT HER ACCUSATIONS ABOUT HIS BEHAVIOUR WITH FRAU K WERE CORRECT.

I'VE BEEN HANDED OVER TO HERR K AS THE PRICE FOR HIS SILENT TOLERATION OF MY FATHER'S AFFAIR WITH K'S WIFE.

MY FATHER ONLY THINKS OF HIS OWN ENJOYMENT AND HAS A GIFT FOR SEEING THINGS IN THE LIGHT WHICH SUITS HIM BEST.

KOF!

KOF! KOF!

This was a characterization which Freud "could not in general dispute". Much as Freud subscribed to Dora's account of the facts, he insisted on a different interpretation of their meaning, one which she was reluctant to accept.

Dora then reported a dream she had previously experienced three nights in succession after Herr K's advance. Freud seized on it as evidence for his case.

Dora's Dream

They hurried downstairs, and as soon as she was outside, Dora woke up. The following day, Dora supplied an addition to her dream – each time after waking up, she smelt smoke.

Fire and Smoke

Freud concluded his interpretation on a triumphalist note.

A kiss with a smoker would certainly smell of smoke. Since Freud frequently remarked "There can be no smoke without fire!", he felt confirmed in his view that the dream had *a special relationship to himself*. Furthermore, Dora's father, Herr K and Freud were all confirmed smokers…

Does it "All Fit"?

Confident in his own subjective experience, Freud knows his judgement is less than convincing to others. Like Dora, we may disagree with his conclusion that it all "fits together very well". There is an overwhelming sense of him striving too hard to make it fit. We do not have to be impressed by his view of Dora's gastric pains or share his enthusiasm for their unlikely cure.

Masturbation then, as now, was common enough and the associated guilt might have correlated with almost any symptom. Freud deserves no bouquets for surmising its presence in his patient. He may even have exacerbated her discomfort by his well-meaning "reassurance".

It does not seem to have occurred to him that the leucorrhea could have been physiological in origin. With his familiar capacity for pushing a good idea too far, Freud comes close to obscuring his own insight in an unconvincing programme of interpretative gymnastics.

Transference and Unconscious Conflict

Yet, if Freud fails to prove his specific points, he nevertheless succeeds in formulating a concept which has proved generally plausible to clinicians and patients alike. Transference, he explains, arises from a whole series of psychological experiences – feelings, phantasies and unconscious impulses rooted in the past.

THESE GHOSTS FROM THE PAST ARE AROUSED AND MADE CONSCIOUS DURING THE PROGRESS OF ANALYSIS...

BUT THEY HAVE THIS PECULIARITY, WHICH IS CHARACTERISTIC FOR THEIR SPECIES, THAT THEY REPLACE SOME **EARLIER** PERSON BY THE **PERSON OF THE PHYSICIAN.**

They result from a hidden personal agenda, a romantic drama in search of its principal performers made manifest in the psychoanalytical situation.

Whatever the reservations concerning Freud's exposition, one thing is strikingly clear – the emotional engagement brought about in the extended one-to-one intimacy of psychoanalytical practice triggered a shift in theoretical concern. Initially, lost memories had been mined in the solitary depths of the individual's unconscious and delivered to the surface in the form of stories about the past.

The nature of the internal world could be divined precisely by paying attention to the relationship between analyst and patient as it unfolded in the consulting room. It was a world of passionate intensity.

The Common Fact of Transference

Freud puts his understanding of transference in the language of libido – impersonal sexual energy. But he saw the origins of transference in a failure of "reality" to satisfy the uniquely personal requirements of an individual's erotic life. This meant that where reality fails, we reinvent it to suit our needs. We create, by means of transference, a love-object conforming to our wishes. In a sense, transference is a kind of dream, a product of the "pleasure principle".

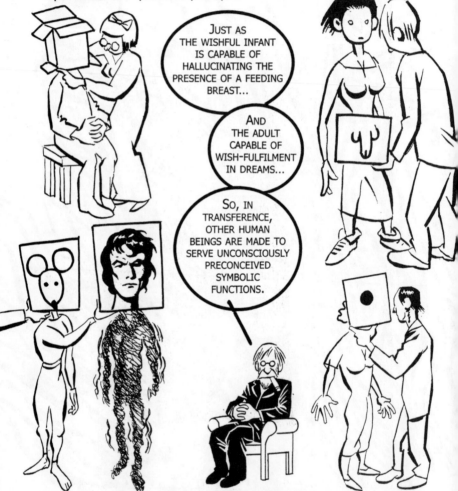

JUST AS THE WISHFUL INFANT IS CAPABLE OF HALLUCINATING THE PRESENCE OF A FEEDING BREAST...

AND THE ADULT CAPABLE OF WISH-FULFILMENT IN DREAMS...

SO, IN TRANSFERENCE, OTHER HUMAN BEINGS ARE MADE TO SERVE UNCONSCIOUSLY PRECONCEIVED SYMBOLIC FUNCTIONS.

"If someone's need for love is not entirely satisfied by reality", Freud explains, "he is bound to approach every new person whom he meets with libidinal anticipatory ideas". Therefore, if total satisfaction is a rare condition, then transference must be common.

Transference is obviously not confined to psychoanalysis but found wherever people come together in any kind of social relation – in families, at work, in school, armies, hospitals, prisons, clubs, associations, etc. Psychoanalysis suggests that we are forever engaged in a kind of "metabolism of meaning".

WE UTILIZE EACH OTHER AS LIVING REPRESENTATIONS OF CHARACTERS AND SCENARIOS ORIGINATING IN OUR UNCONSCIOUS PHANTASIZED WORLD.

WE MODULATE ANXIETY AND FRUSTRATION BY BUILDING OUR OWN PRIVATE THEATRE AND CASTING OTHER PEOPLE - OUR FRIENDS, LOVERS, COLLEAGUES AND FAMILY...

...IN THE ROLES WE WANT THEM TO PLAY.

Nothing causes more pain than the conflict aroused by a failure in this process, a mismatch in casting, a change in our perception of a loved person or a refusal by someone to play their accustomed role. Transference, Freud saw, like culture, was not optional but something in which we are inexorably immersed.

Anatomist of Love

Transference within psychoanalysis occupies a similar position to that of art in society, helping us to know who and what we are. Like art, it inhabits a paradox – evokes real feelings, real impulses, real desires in a setting circumscribed by the conventions of method.

IT DEPENDS ON THE "WILLING SUSPENSION OF DISBELIEF", YET IS CONSTANTLY UNDERMINED BY ABUTTING AGAINST ITS OWN FRAME...

... THE BOUNDARIES OF THE CONSULTATION, THE ANALYST'S FORBEARANCE, THE ATTEMPT TO SHARE UNDERSTANDING OF WISHES RATHER THAN IMPLEMENT THEIR GRATIFICATION.

In focusing his technique on the investigation of transference, Freud had invented a kind of psychological microscope which enabled him to evolve from his origins in neuroanatomy into an anatomist of love.

At the Wheel...

The birth of psychoanalysis was contemporaneous with the development of the petrol-driven motor-car by **G.W. Daimler** (1834-1900). Both inventions were to have profound effects.

The same edition of the *British Medical Journal* in which Freud's ideas were first put forward in England also carried an editorial, "The Therapeutic Possibilities of Automobilism", reporting the beneficial effects of "a properly dosed course of motor driving" on all sufferers from simple anaemia, atonic dyspepsia, gout, neurasthenia and insomnia of nervous origin! As with the future of the car, so we may ask whether and in what form psychoanalysis will survive the new millennium?

Psychoanalytic Knowledge Today

Freud's invention of psychoanalysis must be seen in the context of his time. But can it be taken seriously by intelligent people today? Does anything worthwhile survive? We do not need to dabble in "historical reconstruction" when the activities under discussion are happening now.

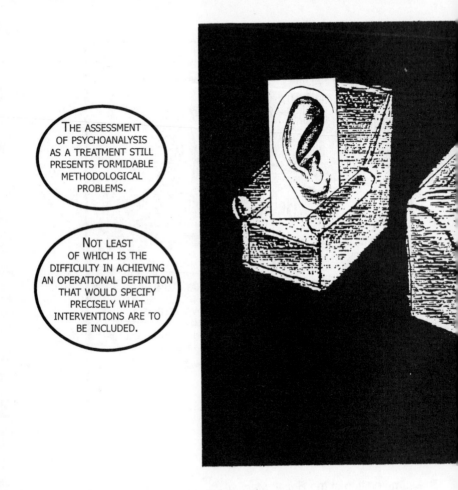

THE ASSESSMENT OF PSYCHOANALYSIS AS A TREATMENT STILL PRESENTS FORMIDABLE METHODOLOGICAL PROBLEMS.

NOT LEAST OF WHICH IS THE DIFFICULTY IN ACHIEVING AN OPERATIONAL DEFINITION THAT WOULD SPECIFY PRECISELY WHAT INTERVENTIONS ARE TO BE INCLUDED.

Psychoanalysis today confronts us not with a monolith but a rag-bag of observations, clinical practices, hypotheses, concepts, metaphors, speculations and theoretical constructions.

Controversies within the psychoanalytic movement have been every bit as acrimonious as those between it and the outside world. Freud's models of the mind – ideas about unconscious functioning – have been elaborated and expanded by psychoanalysts over the years.

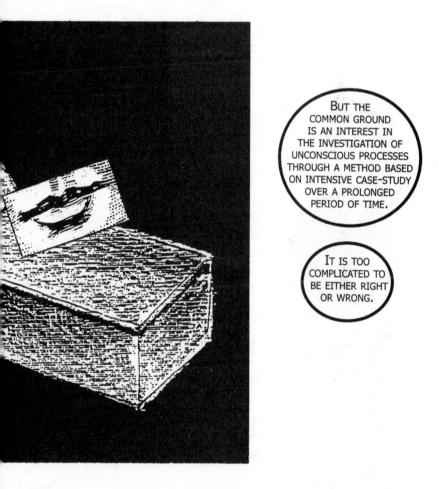

BUT THE COMMON GROUND IS AN INTEREST IN THE INVESTIGATION OF UNCONSCIOUS PROCESSES THROUGH A METHOD BASED ON INTENSIVE CASE-STUDY OVER A PROLONGED PERIOD OF TIME.

IT IS TOO COMPLICATED TO BE EITHER RIGHT OR WRONG.

Psychoanalytic knowledge should derive not from speculation but from the inferences coming out of the consulting room. What are the **rules** which govern such inferences? Psychoanalytic practice is a craft learnt through apprenticeship and only loosely tied to grand theory. But there is a growth of knowledge which seems to depend more on increased conceptual sophistication than the accumulation of "psychological facts". What is the value of this knowledge?

How to Discredit Psychoanalysis?

Psychoanalysis has become a victim of its own success. Critics of Freud often adopt his mode of argument. For instance, this is how Richard Webster explains Freud's admiration for Wilhelm Fliess…

This is typical of critics who discount what they agree with as "not specific to psychoanalysis" and attribute to it only what they find objectionable. Every psychoanalytic truth becomes "something we've always known" and every mistake a "news item" which discredits the whole.

What Unconscious?

There is a more direct way of sabotaging psychoanalysis. This is a fundamental attack on the "unconscious" itself. Freud had an idea that the strategies we develop for self-deception are unconscious mental "defence" mechanisms.

ALTHOUGH MY IDEA HAS WIDESPREAD COMMON-SENSE APPEAL, IT HAS ALWAYS BEEN CHALLENGED. FOR INSTANCE, PROFESSOR MÜNSTERBERG...

THE STORY OF THE SUBCONSCIOUS MIND CAN BE TOLD IN THREE WORDS - THERE IS NONE.

BOOM

Such was the view of Hugo Münsterberg, Professor of Psychology at Harvard University, in his 1910 book *Psychotherapy*.

Münsterberg argued along the lines of French philosopher **René Descartes** (1596-1650).

Unconscious mental activity was therefore "as impossible as a wooden piece of iron". If there is no unconscious mind, then clearly it cannot be analysed, and psychoanalysis must at the very least have misunderstood its subject matter.

Why is Psychoanalysis Controversial?

If psychoanalysis were simply one among a battery of treatments for mental disorder, its founder would be as little known to the general public as are Cerletti and Bini who devised Electroconvulsive Therapy, Cade who discovered the value of Lithium in controlling manic-depressive swings, or the anonymous team of scientists from the Rhone-Poulenc-Spécia laboratories in France who first synthesized the widely used tranquillizer chlorpromazine.

The idea that our behaviour is *unconsciously determined* threatens the rationalist view that we are masters in our own houses. But religion and science itself have delivered a similar determinist message which severely restricts our freedom. It is not the existence of unconscious mental activity nor the recognition of infantile sexual life that people have found hard to stomach.

IT IS THE **CONTENT** THAT I ATTRIBUTE TO THE ADULT UNCONSCIOUS MIND OF SUPPRESSED (INFANTILE) SEXUAL IMPULSES, "PERVERSE" WISHES AND INCESTUOUS DESIRES - THE "**OEDIPUS COMPLEX**".

OUR HANDLING OF THIS COMPLEX IS CRUCIAL TO CHARACTER DEVELOPMENT AND SUBSEQUENT MENTAL HEALTH.

s the Oedipus complex an absurdity or a contribution to our understanding of human sexuality? What is the Oedipus complex?

The original King Oedipus story goes back to a play written by **Sophocles** (c. 496-406 BC) in Ancient Greece.

Oedipus was outcast as a baby because his parents had been warned that he would grow up to murder his father and marry his mother. Oedipus was raised by others that he believed were his parents. He too in early manhood was forewarned of his impending crimes…

And so, to safeguard his (assumed) parents, he fled from them.

He did not realize yet that he had in fact killed his real father and married his own mother.

But it was no dream! When the truth became clear, Oedipus gouged out his eyes and Jocasta hanged herself.

Someone more sceptical than Oedipus might have asked Jocasta two questions...

How can Jocasta be sure that the fear of incest is widespread and that life is easier to bear if we are aware of it *simply as a dream?* Is she offering a pseudo-solution to a pseudo-problem – as Freud himself is accused of doing by inventing a universal "Oedipus complex" that exists only in his own perverse imagination? Let's follow the steps that led Freud to claim the psychological reality of the Oedipus problem...

The "Seduction Theory"

Freud's early theorizing implicated sexual *activity* in the diagnosis of every neurotic disorder. In 1896, he thought that neurasthenia (a syndrome characterized by fatigue, dyspepsia, constipation, loss of libido, etc.) was caused by excessive masturbation, and anxiety neurosis by lack of a satisfactory sexual outlet. But he had a much more complicated account for hysteria and obsessional neurosis.

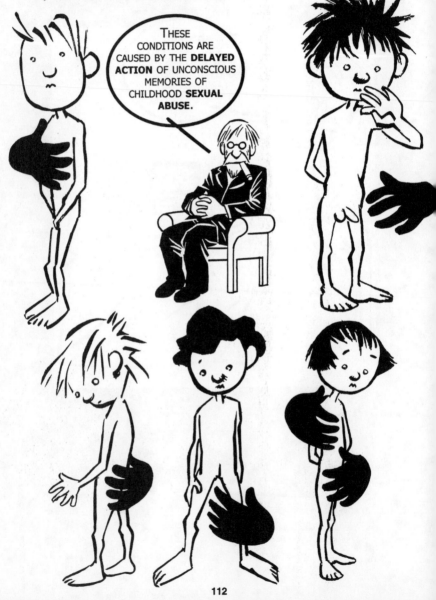

THESE CONDITIONS ARE CAUSED BY THE **DELAYED ACTION** OF UNCONSCIOUS MEMORIES OF CHILDHOOD **SEXUAL ABUSE.**

The action was delayed because the symptoms did not appear at the time when the abuse originally occurred. According to Freud's "seduction theory", it was sexual development at puberty which retroactively invested dormant memories with an intolerably disturbing force that had to be suppressed.

The Return to Memory

Freud had treated 13 cases of hysteria and six cases of obsessional neurosis by the new technique of "psycho-analysis". He discovered (or his critics would say "suggested") a history of forgotten sexual abuse in every case. He even believed his own father to have been a "pervert, responsible for the hysteria of my brother… and those of several younger sisters".

I CAME TO THE CONCLUSION THAT THE DISTRESSING **ANAMNESIS** - THE BRINGING BACK TO MEMORY - OF SEXUAL ABUSE RELEASED PENT-UP FEELINGS AND RELIEVED NEUROTIC SYMPTOMS.

Freud worked hard to elicit these memories which were not spontaneously forthcoming.

For this reason, the accounts obtained (though not necessarily invalid) are open to doubt, as is their putative link to subsequent neurosis. However, the variation between different stories and in the detail reported, make it highly improbable that he suggested them to his patients in any direct way.

True or False Memories?

Freud was clearly aware of the danger of "false memory" and on the lookout for less contaminated evidence. Emma Eckstein – his former patient and now a therapist – was able to supply relevant material from her practice. In December 1897, we find Freud writing to Wilhelm Fliess…

"MY CONFIDENCE IN PATERNAL AETIOLOGY HAS RISEN GREATLY. ECKSTEIN DELIBERATELY TREATED HER PATIENT IN SUCH A MANNER AS NOT TO GIVE HER THE SLIGHTEST HINT OF WHAT WOULD EMERGE FROM THE UNCONSCIOUS AND IN THE PROCESS OBTAINED FROM HER, AMONG OTHER THINGS, THE IDENTICAL SCENES [MEMORIES OF SEXUAL ABUSE] WITH THE FATHER. INCIDENTALLY, THE YOUNG GIRL IS DOING VERY WELL."

In Freud's initial "seduction theory", we can see many of the core elements developed in later psychoanalytic thinking – the notion of *unconscious conflict*, the emphasis on *sexuality*, the belief that *childhood experience* informs adult behaviour, and most importantly, the idea that the emotional significance of *past experience* is transformed through the individual's own programme of biological development.

I INTERPOSED A CONDITIONAL FACTOR - THE EFFECT OF PUBERTY ON UNCONSCIOUS MEMORY TRACES...

...IN ORDER TO EXPLAIN THE DELAY BETWEEN THE CHILDHOOD TRAUMATIC EVENT AND PSYCHOPATHOLOGICAL CONSEQUENCES.

Infantile Sexual Fantasy

Freud had yet to take the crucial and controversial step that would redefine the nature of unconscious mind and its relation to external reality. He would put sexual *fantasy* at centre stage. In September 1897, in a now famous letter, he confessed to Fliess: "I no longer believe in my *neurotica*", by which he meant his seduction theory of the neuroses.

THE CONTINUAL DISAPPOINTMENT IN MY EFFORTS TO BRING A SINGLE ANALYSIS TO A REAL CONCLUSION; THE RUNNING AWAY OF PEOPLE WHO FOR A PERIOD OF TIME HAD BEEN MOST GRIPPED BY ANALYSIS; THE ABSENCE OF THE COMPLETE SUCCESSES ON WHICH I HAD COUNTED; THE POSSIBILITY OF EXPLAINING TO MYSELF THE PARTIAL SUCCESSES IN OTHER WAYS, IN THE USUAL FASHION - THIS WAS THE FIRST GROUP.

All Pervert Fathers?

THEN THE SURPRISE THAT IN ALL CASES THE **FATHER**, NOT EXCLUDING MY OWN, HAD TO BE ACCUSED OF BEING PERVERSE – THE REALIZATION OF THE UNEXPECTED FREQUENCY OF HYSTERIA, WITH PRECISELY THE SAME CONDITIONS PREVAILING IN EACH, WHEREAS SURELY SUCH WIDESPREAD PERVERSIONS AGAINST CHILDREN ARE NOT VERY PROBABLE. THE INCIDENCE OF PERVERSION WOULD HAVE TO BE IMMEASURABLY MORE FREQUENT THAN THE RESULTING HYSTERIA BECAUSE THE ILLNESS AFTER ALL OCCURS ONLY WHEN THERE HAS BEEN AN ACCUMULATION OF EVENTS AND THERE IS A CONTRIBUTING FACTOR THAT WEAKENS THE DEFENCE.

The Fantasy Factor

THEN, THIRD, THE CERTAIN INSIGHT THAT THERE ARE **NO INDICATIONS OF REALITY IN THE UNCONSCIOUS**, SO THAT ONE CANNOT DISTINGUISH BETWEEN TRUTH AND FICTION THAT HAS BEEN CATHECTED (MENTAL ENERGY CONCENTRATED INTO ONE CHANNEL) WITH AFFECT (FEELING ATTACHED TO AN IDEA).

ACCORDINGLY, THERE WOULD REMAIN THE SOLUTION THAT THE SEXUAL FANTASY INVARIABLY SEIZES UPON THE THEME OF PARENTS.

Bearing in mind that the seduction theory required early sexual abuse as a necessary precondition in *every case*, Freud's three reasons might seem sufficiently compelling to raise doubts concerning at least some of the memories, and thus to undermine it.

But not for Jeffrey Masson, author of the still controversial book *The Assault on Truth* (1984), who accuses Freud of suppressing scenes of sexual abuse rather than inventing them. Masson's own position as distinguished translator and editor of the Freud–Fliess correspondence gave him the apparent status of "expert witness" in the case against Freud.

FREUD **KNEW** THE SEDUCTION THEORY WAS TRUE BUT REPUDIATED IT TO PACIFY CRITICAL COLLEAGUES AND CONFORM TO PREVAILING SOCIAL PREJUDICES...

FREUD CHANGED HIS MIND NOT FOR THEORETICAL OR CLINICAL REASONS BUT BECAUSE OF A PERSONAL FAILURE OF COURAGE.

Did Freud Suppress Evidence?

Masson's argument is unlikely. In the first place, notwithstanding his doubts, Freud continued to entertain his original theory and subscribe to it in published material.

IT WAS NOT UNTIL 1905, A FULL EIGHT YEARS AFTER MY NEUROTICA LETTER TO FLIESS, THAT I PUBLICLY CONFIRMED MY EARLY OVERESTIMATION OF THE FREQUENCY OF CHILDHOOD SEXUAL SEDUCTION...

... AND EVEN THEN, I TOOK THE TROUBLE TO EMPHASIZE THE REALITY OF ITS OCCURRENCE.

Did Freud Cover Up For Abusive Fathers?

However, in exculpating his father, Freud provided further grounds for speculation about his purpose in distancing himself from the seduction theory. Both Marianne Krüll in *Freud and His Father* (1986) and Marie Balmary in *Psychoanalyzing Psychoanalysis: Freud and the Hidden Fault of the Father* (1982) anticipate Masson in imputing personal rather than professional motives.

IT WAS AN UNWARRANTED ATTEMPT TO SHIFT THE BLAME FOR NEUROSIS AWAY FROM FATHERS (AND PARENTS IN GENERAL) ONTO THE CHILDREN THEMSELVES.

MY FATHER'S MISDEMEANOURS PROVIDED GROUNDS FOR EXTRAVAGANT SPECULATION.

ADULTERY, MASTURBATION AND LOSS OF FAITH IN JUDAISM...

... AND THE PROVOCATION OF HIS SECOND WIFE'S SUICIDE CAN BE ADDED TO THE LIST OF THINGS FREUD COULDN'T FACE ABOUT HIS FATHER.

Let's suppose that Freud was driven by social pressure or filial loyalty or moral cowardice into dishonesty. But, as Masson himself points out, Freud felt most isolated and vulnerable in 1896 when he first announced the seduction theory.

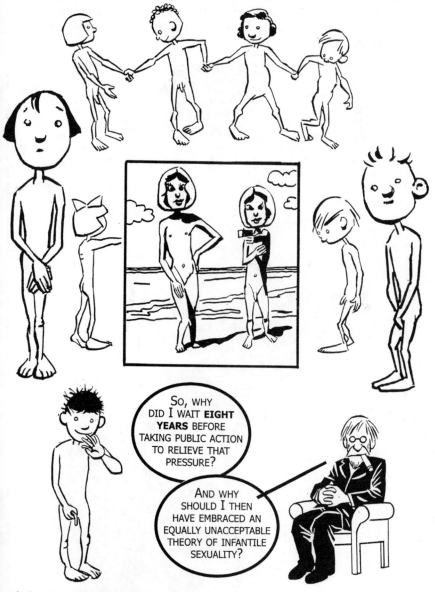

So, why did I wait **EIGHT YEARS** before taking public action to relieve that pressure?

And why should I then have embraced an equally unacceptable theory of infantile sexuality?

Is it not more likely that Freud simply remained uncertain about a complex matter that was difficult to resolve?

Beyond Sexual Abuse

Robert Paul clarifies the issue in his cogently argued rebuttal of Masson ("Freud and the Seduction Theory", 1985): *"Freud never ceased to believe that girls were often seduced by their fathers or uncles or older brothers, nor that this could very well lead them into neurosis; but he did cease to believe that such seductions were the **necessary** and **sufficient** cause of hysteria."*

Self-Analysis and Sexual Fantasy

What led Freud to become convinced that, apart from the reality of sexual seduction in childhood, "sexual fantasy invariably seized on the theme of the parents"? What induced him to posit a universal psychology that privileged unconscious sexual myth over everyday memory?

It was his excursion into self-analysis – the sub-text he derived from his own dreams, that clinched the issue. And it came to a head during the summer of 1897, in the year following his father's death.

In the Looking-Glass

That summer Freud was in a bad state. His mood was fluctuating wildly from high to low, he was preoccupied with feelings of impotence, failure and guilt, and suffered an inhibiting intellectual paralysis which interfered with his researches. He was on the verge of a breakdown. At the same time, he was involved in treating a young man with whom he had much in common. Like Freud, this patient was suffering with a severe reaction to the loss of his father.

HE'D BECOME CRIPPLED WITH OBSESSIONAL FEARS, BELIEVING THAT HE WOULD GO INTO THE STREET AND MURDER THE FIRST PERSON HE ENCOUNTERED.

I INSIST THAT MY HOUSEKEEPER LOCK ME IN AT NIGHT SO I CAN'T GET OUT AND COMMIT MURDER IN A SOMNAMBULISTIC STATE...

During his analysis, which was apparently successful, this man recalled having murderous impulses in childhood towards his over-severe father. He had wanted to push him over a mountain precipice!

HIS OBSESSIONAL FEAR OF MURDERING STRANGERS APPEARED AS A DISGUISE, REPLACING HIS FATHER - THE UNDERSTANDABLE BUT UNACCEPTABLE OBJECT OF HIS REAL HOSTILITY - WITH AN INEXPLICABLE SYMPTOM.

I ALSO DREAM OF INCESTUOUS ACTS WITH MY MOTHER...

Both these wishes completed the Oedipal configuration. But all this might have struck Freud as a unique item of abnormal psychology, had he not found himself identifying so closely with the young man.

Freud's Dream

While this case was fresh in his mind, Freud made a long journey. He was travelling first class in a crowded train. When he entered his compartment, an elderly aristocratic-looking couple were obviously irritated by his arrival.

The woman put her umbrella on the window-seat opposite, so that Freud could not sit there. Finally, adding insult to injury, when the ticket collector came round and Freud showed the ticket he had bought at great expense, he discovered that the couple were travelling on some kind of free pass!

At this point, Freud fell asleep and had a dream. In the first part of the dream, he heard the nonsensical name *"Hollthurn, ten minutes"* being called out.

In the dream, he now found himself in a different carriage, and still in the dream explained it to himself...

Freud's Analysis of His Dream

Freud noticed that like his obsessional patient, he had been preoccupied with *sleep-walking*. But what about the young man's incestuous dream and his hostility towards his father? Freud now offers a fantastical explanation for the stand-offish manner in which the elderly couple had treated him.

The familiar theme of intrusion into the parental bedroom emerges here. It comes as no surprise to hear Freud announcing in a letter to Fliess that he has found, "in my own case too, [the phenomenon of] being in love with my mother and jealous of my father".

Early Sexual Trauma

This is how Freud summed up the idea three years later in
The Interpretation of Dreams...

*"It is the fate of all of us, perhaps, to direct our first sexual impulses
towards our mother and our first hatred and our first murderous wish
against our father. Our dreams convince us that this is so. King Oedipus,
who slew his father Laius and married his mother Jocasta, merely
shows us the fulfilment of our own childhood wishes."*

BUT MORE FORTUNATE THAN HE, WE HAVE MEANWHILE SUCCEEDED, IN SO FAR AS WE HAVE NOT BECOME PSYCHONEUROTICS, IN DETACHING OUR SEXUAL IMPULSES FROM OUR MOTHERS AND IN FORGETTING OUR JEALOUSY OF OUR FATHERS.

Far from denying the importance of early sexual trauma, if Freud's view were correct, it would provide an account of how such trauma creates psychological damage.

In fact, it was precisely the way in which these processes were accomplished – the developmental task involved in relinquishing a passionate attachment to parents - that soon became the keystone for a new theory of character development.

The Process of Internalization

The Oedipus complex, Freud thought, led inexorably towards the internalization of parents as a response to the experience of loss. What he did was to link up two lines of observation.

In both cases, the loved person is unconsciously preserved as a psychological entity in the mind of the bereaved.

It was the work of mourning in adults, and the grief involved in surrendering exclusive rights to parental love in children, that established internal figures in place of the relinquished ones in the outside world.

WHAT HAD BEEN THE OBJECT – THE PARENT **OUT THERE** – IS TRANSFORMED UNCONSCIOUSLY INTO A COMPONENT OF THE SUBJECT – THE PARENT **IN THERE.**

Henceforth, this internalization exercized influence over the personality from its new psychological locus. In short, the inter-personal was rendered *intra*-personal.

Identification and Fantasy

The psychoanalytic model of the mind now came to envisage its growth through the acquisition of **identifications** – psychological versions of people in the outside world which carry standards, values, interests and qualities of character.

BUT THE CHARACTERISTICS OF THESE "INNER VERSIONS" ARE MODIFIED AND DISTORTED BY THE INDIVIDUAL'S OWN ARCHAIC MODES OF PERCEPTION.

In this way, these internal figures become increasingly different from their external counterparts – they have *fantasized* qualities assigned to them from a range of heroes and villains.

By the mid-1920s, this elaborated view of the Oedipus complex, with all its consequences for an understanding of human development, had become essential to psychoanalytical thinking. Freud was able to assert...

Against the Oedipus Complex

In today's post-Freudian world, it is difficult to gauge the "moral shock" and "extreme disgust" first produced by Freud's exposition of the Oedipus complex. Modern opponents of psychoanalysis are more likely to entrench themselves in the paradoxical claim that the Oedipal theory is both *untestable* and *demonstrably untrue*.

Let us take a closer look at the case against the Oedipus complex as presented by **Frederick Crews** (*The Memory Wars*, NYREV: 1995, p. 122). Crews tells us that well-designed experimental studies have not produced a shred of evidence to substantiate it.

Frederick Crews

H.J.Eysenck

HE DOES NOT DESCRIBE THE NEGATIVE EVIDENCE BUT INSTEAD REFERS US TO EYSENCK WHOSE STANDARDS OF SCIENTIFIC RESEARCH HE ADMIRES.

IF WE NOW ASK EYSENCK TO SUPPLY HIS EVIDENCE, HE PRODUCES NO "WELL-DESIGNED EXPERIMENTS" BUT THE HAPHAZARD IMPRESSIONS DERIVED FROM OBSERVATIONS OF HIS OWN FIVE CHILDREN GROWING UP.

The anti-Oedipus company is thus a precarious pyramid of acrobats resting on the shoulders of one man.

Valentine's Experiments

What well-designed experiments did Valentine carry out? None, only a trivial and badly designed one. Like Eysenck, he observed his own (also five) children, but he made detailed notes on two of them, a boy B and a girl Y. Both children showed a marked preference for their mother from an early age.

From the age of about two-and-a-half, Valentine's children showed increasing affection towards their father. At three years and two months, the little boy would argue with and tease his mother, but not his father.

Interesting though these observations are, they scarcely constitute hard evidence against the Oedipus complex. Valentine takes it for granted that unconscious jealousy would manifest itself in his children's overt expressions of antagonism, rather than enhanced expressions of care and concern that "protest too much". He also conflates the manifestations of "identification" with those of object-love.

WHEN HE NOTICES THAT AFTER THE AGE OF TWO OR THREE THE TASTES OF HIS CHILDREN ARE MORE IN-LINE WITH THE **SAME-SEX** PARENT, HE TAKES IT AS A SIGN OF AFFECTION REFUTING OEDIPAL JEALOUSY, RATHER THAN AS A SIGN OF IDENTIFICATION RESULTING FROM IT.

Experiment in Simple Curiosity

Valentine recognized that his observations could not be taken as an adequate basis for generalization. He designed a questionnaire concerning children which he circulated to 16 friends specially selected for their supposed neutrality towards Freud. Not surprisingly, the results broadly confirmed his own opinions, with one exception.

FAMILY 16 DID NOT SUBSCRIBE TO MY HYPOTHESIS THAT CHILDREN'S INTEREST IN SEXUAL MATTERS IS A SIMPLE FUNCTION OF THEIR CURIOSITY ABOUT THE FORBIDDEN.

BUT THEN THESE PARENTS TURNED OUT TO BE "CRYPTO-FREUDIANS", SO WE ARE TO ASSUME THEY DO NOT COUNT.

If we accept the sceptical argument which discounts the accumulated clinical experience of psychoanalytic practitioners, on the grounds that it is subject to self-serving distortions, we must by the same token reject the reports of Valentine and his friends regarding their own children.

Valentine did carry out one so-called "empirical" experiment on his children. He placed a small empty box on a shelf which he instructed them not to open.

QUESTIONS ABOUT THE CONTENTS OF THE BOX CONTINUED FOR SEVERAL DAYS, AND IN THE CASE OF THE YOUNGEST CHILD, SEVERAL WEEKS.

HE DOES NOT SAY EXACTLY HOW LONG HE WAITED BEFORE DISAPPOINTING THEM BY REVEALING ITS EMPTINESS.

THIS EXPERIMENT CONFIRMS WHAT WE ALL KNOW – THAT INTEREST IN GENERAL CAN BE STIMULATED BY PROHIBITION.

But it does not follow that this is a sufficient explanation for a child's interest in sex. There was of course no "control box", so we do not know how much longer his children would have remained interested in a box which when opened always provided a *pleasurable* stimulus.

Evidence of the Oedipus Complex

There is empirical evidence which suggests that the Oedipus complex exists and is a pervasive feature of human development. Jocasta (and Freud) were right: men do dream and always have dreamt both of incest and patricide. **Plato** (c. 428-347 BC) had already commented on this in his *Republic*.

IN SLEEP THE WILD BEAST IN US, FULL-FED WITH MEAT OR DRINK, BECOMES RAMPANT AND SHAKES OFF SLEEP TO GO IN QUEST OF WHAT WILL GRATIFY ITS OWN INSTINCTS...

IN PHANTASY IT WILL NOT SHRINK FROM INTERCOURSE WITH A MOTHER OR ANYONE ELSE, MAN, GOD, OR BRUTE, OR FROM FORBIDDEN FOOD OR ANY DEED OF BLOOD.

Freud has taught us that such transgressions are more often *indirectly* expressed. **Robert Louis Stevenson** (1850-94), famous for his *Treasure Island*, wrote an essay *On Dreams* shortly after his father's death and first published in 1892, eight years before the publication of Freud's *Interpretation of Dreams*.

Stevenson's Dream

In this dream, Stevenson is the son of a rich, bad tempered and wicked man. He has avoided his father by living abroad for years. On returning to England he discovers his father has remarried a young wife. For some reason (which the dreamer indistinctly understands), it is desirable for father and son to meet.

His father's widow then discovers his crime but refrains from denouncing him.

And this precipitates the dreamer's instantaneous awakening.

Stevenson's dream is unmistakably Oedipal. The only concession to propriety is the flimsy device of turning his mother into his father's *second* wife. Those critics who accept Freud's insight into himself and his own culture – but challenge the general applicability of his findings – must therefore include late-19th-century Scottish Calvinists like Stevenson together with Viennese Jews and Ancient Greeks in the Oedipus club.

Calvin Hall and colleagues studying more than 10,000 dreams were able to confirm the pattern in American college students in the 1960s. William N. Stephens in *The Oedipus Complex: Cross-cultural Evidence* found persuasive indications in Amerindian communities indicating that young boys become sexually attracted to their mothers, and that this attraction could generate lasting sexual fears and avoidances.

Oedipus in the Trobriand Islands

The Trobriand Islanders, studied by **Bronislaw Malinowski** (1884-1942) in his classic book *Sex and Repression in Savage Society* (1927), were long held to be an exception to the Oedipal rule due to their matrilineal kinship pattern. Malinowski argued that uncles not fathers have authority over children in the Trobriands.

BOYS DEVELOP A "MATRILINEAL COMPLEX", TAKING THEIR SISTER AS LIBIDINAL OBJECT AND DIRECTING THEIR AGGRESSION TOWARDS THE MOTHER'S BROTHER.

But a careful re-analysis of Malinowski's data led the anthropologist Melford Spiro to conclude that there was little evidence for a matrilineal complex in the Trobriands and strong evidence for an Oedipus complex.

Malinowski had described the Trobrianders as a people of "strong passions and complex sentiments". Still, Spiro was surprised by what he found: *"... I did not anticipate the extreme degree to which the wish to recapitulate the Oedipal triangle in the Trobriands would extend. Almost all marriages in the Trobriands are monogamous, polygyny – a mark of wealth, power, and prestige – being practised only by chiefs. That the sons of chiefs are as adulterous as the sons of commoners is not surprising."*

WHAT IS SURPRISING, HOWEVER, IS THAT THEY TYPICALLY SEEK (AND FIND) THEIR PARAMOURS FROM AMONG THEIR FATHER'S WIVES (EXCEPTING, OF COURSE, THEIR OWN MOTHERS).

What Robert Louis Stevenson could only dream of, the (supposedly non-Oedipal) Trobrianders turn out to regularly enact!

Complexity of the Oedipus Complex

There can be little doubt that what anthropologists refer to as the "motivational disposition to nuclear family incest" is a pan-human phenomenon. To recognize this, however, is not necessarily to subscribe to Freud's Oedipus complex which distinguishes the adherents of psychoanalysis from its opponents. If Freud began by acknowledging the theme of disposition to incest, he very soon elaborated a series of variations on its psychological consequences.

These concepts are woven into a package of theories that touch on character formation, gender differentiation, sexual orientation and the aetiology of neurotic symptoms.

If we look at what the Oedipus complex has grown to imply over the years, we discover not one but many "complexes". And all of them are controversial.

1. We have the complex as manifest in adult dreams and the complex as manifest in children's play.

2. The overt expression of the complex and the subtle symbolic expression of the complex.

3. The complex in the consulting room and the cross-cultural complex.

4. The negative complex (a girl's attachment to father and rivalry with mother) and the positive complex.

5. The complex in early infancy and the complex in later childhood.

6. The complex as a chronological phase of development and the complex as a state of mind.

7. The generalized complex (any triangular object-relationship) and the specific complex.

8. The phylogenetic complex and the socially determined complex.

9. The counter-Oedipal complex (the parents' own wishes, desires and behaviour towards the child).

The very fecundity of the idea within psychoanalytic thinking has created a moving target for those who seek to pin it down. The progressive "complexification" of the Oedipus complex has brought us to the point, the psychoanalyst Bennet Simon says, where the concept is so rich that it is in danger of losing its specificity. In post-Freudian psychoanalysis there is no shibboleth, only the multiplicity of interpretations to which it gave rise.

The Problem of Gender Identity

Freud accepted the common fact that sexual desire is founded on a bedrock of biological necessity – part of our animal inheritance and the natural functioning of our bodies. He also noted the now uncontroversial fact that infants derive pleasure from the manipulation of their genitals. But he went further…

THIS MASTURBATORY ACTIVITY IS ACCOMPANIED BY MENTAL REPRESENTATIONS IN WHICH THEIR PARENTS FIGURE…

FROM CLINICAL EXPERIENCE, I CONCLUDE THAT THE PSYCHOLOGICAL ASPECTS OF ADULT SEXUALITY DERIVE FROM EARLY PASSIONATE RELATIONSHIPS WITH MOTHER AND FATHER – THE "OEDIPUS COMPLEX".

Our adult gender identity and choice of sex-object depend upon the complex play of unconscious forces at work in the infant.

Environmental circumstances also played a part, but Freud was unsure just how these interacted with the psycho-biological programme. For instance, such factors as…

THE PARENTS' ATTEMPTS TO SUPPRESS INFANTILE MASTURBATION

TOILET TRAINING

THE WITNESSING OF PARENTAL INTERCOURSE IN WHICH THE FATHER'S PENIS "DISAPPEARS" INTO THE MOTHER'S BODY

Although each person followed his or her unique developmental pathway, Freud tried to delineate a "typical" history of unconscious psychological development for each sex.

The Making of Masculinity

Freud saw the development of masculinity as relatively unproblematic.

1. The mother's feeding breast and the mother herself are the baby's first love objects.

2. They remain unconsciously represented in the young man's later attraction to women.

3. The penis, originally thought to be an attribute of both sexes, comes to represent power and strength.

4. It was clearly a good thing to have.

But the little boy's first knowledge of the anatomical distinction between the sexes was filled with anxiety. It confirms a pre-existing unconscious fear of castration – part of his evolutionary inheritance!

Castration Anxiety

The sight of the female genitals witnessed the existence of a species of being who had been so deprived. It was therefore possible for his (pleasure-giving) penis to be lost... most likely cut off by the chief rival for his mother's affection – his father. This is the "castration anxiety" that boys undergo.

MY APPREHENSION OF THE FEMALE AS "CASTRATED MALE" LEADS ME TO A HORROR OF BEING LIKE WOMEN.

BUT IT ALSO DRIVES THE LITTLE BOY TO WITHDRAW HIS LIBIDINAL ATTACHMENT FROM PARENTS AND REINSTALL THEM IN HIS MIND AS **INNER FIGURES** - COMPONENTS OF THE CONSCIENCE OR "SUPER-EGO".

The Super-Ego

The super-ego, Freud thought, was composed of "a precipitate of abandoned object-cathexes [attachments]".

And Femininity... ?

Freud found it difficult to understand female psychology, which he characterized as a "dark continent". He famously remarked to his friend, Princess Marie Bonaparte…

THE GREAT QUESTION THAT HAS NEVER BEEN ANSWERED AND WHICH I HAVE NOT YET BEEN ABLE TO ANSWER, DESPITE MY 30 YEARS OF RESEARCH INTO THE FEMININE SOUL, IS "WHAT DOES A WOMAN WANT?"

What is Femininity?

Because all babies begin their emotional and sexual lives with a profound attachment to mother and derive sensual pleasure from manipulation of their own genitals (in the girl's case, clitoral stimulation), Freud asked himself how adult femininity was achieved.

If infantile experience was the model for later sexuality, how did the girl-child come to transfer her affections to members of the opposite sex, and how did she acquire the wish for vaginal penetration? These questions puzzled Freud.

The Female Response to Castration Anxiety

Listening to his female patients, especially perhaps his own daughter, Anna, who was a case in point, Freud concluded that the little girl's first sight of the male genital led to a wish that it should be part of herself.

Girls are inclined to see their mothers as representatives of an inferior status. Only when this had been overcome – when the desire to be a man had been transformed into the desire to *contain* one, and thence into the desire for motherhood – can she progress to a truly feminine position.

A Prejudicial View of Women

Freud's fondness for grand theory led him into sweeping, prejudicial and untenable generalizations. His Oedipal theory dictated that the female response to castration anxiety would *not* drive the little girl to relinquish her libidinal attachment to father and would not therefore result in the early internalization of a super-ego.

AS A RESULT, WOMEN LACK THE MORAL CONSCIENCE OF MEN...

BY DISPLACEMENT OF THEIR "PENIS-ENVY", THEY ARE MORE PRONE TO JEALOUSY IN ALL SORTS OF OTHER WAYS.

The wish to be like a man – the "masculine protest" – might easily derive from a realistic aspiration to enjoy the advantageous social status accorded to men.

Yet Freud's treatment of female friends and colleagues belied his theoretical misogyny. He encouraged their admission into early psychoanalytic societies and respected their contributions to the movement. They were not slow to challenge his ideas on female psychology. **Karen Horney** (1885-1952) was among the first in a series of brilliant papers published between 1920 and the mid-1930s, now collected in her book *Feminine Psychology* (1967).

IN THIS FORMULATION WE HAVE ASSUMED AS AN AXIOMATIC FACT THAT FEMALES FEEL AT A DISADVANTAGE BECAUSE OF THEIR GENITAL ORGANS, WITHOUT THIS BEING REGARDED AS A PROBLEM IN ITSELF — PROBABLY BECAUSE TO MASCULINE NARCISSISM THIS HAS SEEMED TOO SELF-EVIDENT TO NEED EXPLANATION.

NEVERTHELESS, THE CONCLUSION SO FAR DRAWN FROM THE INVESTIGATIONS — AMOUNTING AS IT DOES TO AN ASSERTION THAT ONE HALF OF THE HUMAN RACE IS DISCONTENTED WITH THE SEX ASSIGNED TO IT AND CAN OVERCOME THIS DISCONTENT ONLY IN FAVOURABLE CIRCUMSTANCES...

... IS DECIDEDLY UNSATISFYING, NOT ONLY TO FEMALE NARCISSISM BUT ALSO TO BIOLOGICAL SCIENCE.

Breast-Envy

Melanie Klein, who together with Anna Freud pioneered child-psychoanalysis, managed to cap Freud's theory of penis-envy by postulating an earlier and more profound form of envy from which it derived – breast-envy! In so doing she rescued psychoanalysis from its anti-feminist bias.

YES... PENIS-ENVY AND THE CASTRATION COMPLEX PLAY AN IMPORTANT PART IN THE GIRL'S DEVELOPMENT...

BUT THEY DERIVE FROM AN EARLIER ENVY, SHARED BY BOTH SEXES, OF THE MOTHER'S INEXHAUSTIBLE BREAST.

ONLY LATER IS THIS TRANSFERRED ONTO THE PATERNAL ORGAN.

Early Origin of the Super-Ego

Klein challenged the notion of a "phallic woman", and the subsequent disillusion and disappointment in her own genital lack, as being far less important than Freud believed. The feminine desire to internalize the penis arose directly from her genital make-up and invariably preceded any wish to possess a penis of her own.

BESIDES WHICH, THE INTERNALIZATION OF "IDENTIFICATIONS" BEGINS EARLIER IN THE CHILD'S LIFE THAN FREUD SUPPOSES...

THESE GIVE RISE TO A PRIMITIVE SUPER-EGO WHICH IS **NOT** DRIVEN BY CASTRATION ANXIETY.

None of the conclusions concerning women's moral capacity would therefore follow. If the little girl turned away from her mother, it was more because she phantasized mother as containing father's penis and his babies than because of any supposed "lack" of a phallus.

Freud's Views on Homosexuality

A similar cleavage between theory and practice characterizes Freud's attitude towards homosexuality, which he comes to see as linked with paranoia. Yet he also believed that there was an unconscious *universal* human bisexuality underlying our sexual development. "Perverse" additions to the "normal sexual aim" were ubiquitous and made the word "perversion" inappropriate as a term of reproach. How did Freud attempt to fit homosexual object choice into his Oedipal Theory?

THE MALE CHILD RESPONDS TO CASTRATION ANXIETY BY TRYING TO PRESERVE THE FANTASIZED NOTION OF A "PHALLIC MOTHER".

HE THEREFORE CHOOSES A COMPROMISE FIGURE - A BOY OR YOUNG MAN WITH FEMININE FEATURES.

OR PERHAPS HE ATTEMPTS TO PRESERVE HIS BOND WITH MOTHER BY INTRODUCING HER INTO HIS "EGO" - UNCONSCIOUSLY IDENTIFYING WITH HER AND THEN CHOOSING FUTURE LOVE-OBJECTS WHO RESEMBLE HIMSELF.

Homophobia and Latent Homosexuality

Freud thought that homophobia, the fear and denial of a person's own homosexual leanings, led to hatred of the same-sex love-object. It was as if a man said to himself, "No, I do not love him. Actually I hate him."

ONCE THE HATRED IS ESTABLISHED, THEN A REASON FOR IT HAS TO BE INVENTED...

SO THAT THE FORMULA BECOMES: "I HATE HIM BECAUSE HE PERSECUTES ME."

This theory established a link between "latent" homosexuality and the development of paranoia.

Freud's Support For Homosexuals

Freud did not believe that homosexuality as such was a mental illness. In 1903, he wrote in the *Die Zeit* newspaper, "I am... of the firm conviction that homosexuals must not be treated as sick people, for a perverse orientation is far from being a sickness. Would that not oblige us to characterize as sick many great thinkers and scholars of all times... ?"

In 1921, together with the analyst **Otto Rank** (1884-1939), he wrote to his future biographer **Ernest Jones** (1879-1958) on the subject of whether homosexuals should be allowed to train as psychoanalysts. "Your query, dear Ernest, concerning prospective membership of homosexuals has been considered by us and we disagree with you. In effect, we cannot exclude such persons without other sufficient reasons, as we cannot agree with their legal persecution. We feel that a decision in such cases should depend upon a thorough examination of the other qualities of the candidate."

Freud championed the cause of decriminalizing homosexuality at a time when it was widely proscribed. In 1930, he was a co-signatory to a public appeal in Austria and Germany. Five years later, in a "Letter to an American Mother" who enquired what help psychoanalysis might provide for her son, he wrote: "By asking me if I can help, you mean, I suppose, if I can abolish homosexuality and make normal heterosexuality take its place. The answer is, in a general way, we cannot promise to achieve it... What analysis can do for your son runs in a different line. If he is unhappy, torn by conflicts, inhibited by his social life, analysis may bring him harmony, peace of mind, full efficiency, whether he remains a homosexual or gets changed... Homosexuality is assuredly no advantage, but it is nothing to be ashamed of, no vice, no degradation, it cannot be classified as an illness; we consider it to be a variation of sexual functioning produced by a certain arrest of sexual development."

Freud and God

Throughout his life, Freud was a militant atheist. He refused to let his wife, brought up as an orthodox Jew, light the sabbath candles. He threatened to turn Protestant rather than participate in a Jewish marriage ceremony. Yet, it is interesting that Freud's father, Jacob Freud, inscribed a Bible in Hebrew and gave it to his unregenerate son on the occasion of his 35th birthday.

It was the same Philippson Bible from which his father had probably read him stories in his childhood, and it was decorated with woodcuts coloured in with a childish hand, probably Freud's.

Shortly after his father's death in 1896, Freud became a compulsive collector of antiquities. He filled his study with ancient figurines and had them permanently lined up on his desk. He felt comforted by their presence and referred to them fondly, as if they were real people.

They remained with him till the day he died, when he bequeathed them to his daughter, Anna.

There is a remarkable resemblance between these ancient objects and the ones depicted in the woodcuts in the Philippson Bible that Freud's father gave him. So, was Freud's love for these objects a kind of distorted religious experience or idol worship?

Applying his own ideas concerning self-deception – to the effect that repressed memories can be turned into actions – Ana-María Rizzuto in *Why Did Freud Reject God* (1998) suggests that his disposition to collect was a way of evoking fond memories of Bible study with his father – and by extension, benign providence. It was, she suggests, a suppressed form of religious devotion.

Further Reading

S. Wilson, *Sigmund Freud*, Sutton Publishing, 1997. Very succinct and accessible account of Freud's life and ideas. Can be read in one hour.

M. Macmillan, *Freud Evaluated: The Completed Arc*, MIT Press, 1997. Detailed critique (762 pages) of the origin and validity of Freud's psychoanalytic ideas by an academic psychologist.

S. Fisher and R.P. Greenberg, *Freud Scientifically Reappraised: Testing the Theories and Therapy*, John Wiley & Sons, 1996; and *The Scientific Credibility of Freud's Theories and Therapy*, Columbia University Press, 1985. Dispassionate reviews of the empirical evidence bearing on Freud's theories by two academic psychologists.

A. Petocz, *Freud, Psychoanalysis and Symbolism*, Cambridge University Press, 1999. Lucid exposition of a scientifically acceptable theory of symbolism that can be derived from Freud's work, by a philosopher and psychologist.

H. Eysenck, *Decline and Fall of the Freudian Empire*, Viking, 1985; Pelican, 1986; Penguin, 1991. Classic anti-Freudian polemic by a research psychologist.

J.M. Masson, *The Assault on Truth: Freud's Suppression of the Seduction Theory*, Faber & Faber, 1984; Farrar, Straus & Giroux, 1984; Penguin, 1985; Fontana, 1992. Apostate psychoanalyst suggests that Freud deliberately obscured the importance of childhood sexual abuse in causing mental disorder by inventing a false theory of unconscious sexual fantasy.

F. Crews et al., *The Memory Wars: Freud's Legacy in Dispute*, The New York Review of Books, 1995. Two essays attacking Freudian psychoanalysis by a professor of literature, together with responses from critics, first published in the *New York Review of Books* in 1993 and 1994. Argues against the recovered-memory movement and charges Freud with inventing memories of childhood sexual abuse in his patients and thus overemphasizing their importance in the aetiology of mental disorder.

S. Frosh, *For and Against Psychoanalysis*, Routledge, 1997. An academic and clinical psychologist attempts a balanced appraisal of psychoanalysis as theory and therapy.

T. Szasz, *Anti-Freud: Karl Kraus's Criticism of Psychoanalysis and Psychiatry*, Syracuse University Press, 1976, 1990. Veteran anti-psychiatrist of the 1960s and 70s collects the acerbic criticisms levelled at Freud by contemporary Viennese writer and satirist. Argues that psychoanalysis is not a scientific "therapy" but a species of "conversation" – a human relationship or mode of spiritual healing.

E. Gellner, *The Psychoanalytic Movement: The Cunning of Unreason*, Paladin, 1985; Fontana, 1993; Northwestern University Press, 2000. Argues psychoanalysis gives a naturalistic yet false account of the "dark side" of human nature. Witty socio-historical analysis of why this should be appealing.

J. Lear, *Love and its Place in Nature: A Philosophical Interpretation of Freudian Psychoanalysis*, Farrar, Straus & Giroux, 1990; Noonday Press, 1991; Yale University Press, 1999. Philosopher sees psychoanalysis as a celebration of the individual, and psychoanalytic cure as a manifestation of the power of love.

J. Bouveresse, *Wittgenstein Reads Freud: The Myth of the Unconscious*, Princeton University Press, 1995, 1996. Collection of Ludwig Wittgenstein's clear and not so clear thoughts concerning Freud. "Unless you think *very* clearly, psychoanalysis is a dangerous and foul practice... All this, of course, doesn't detract from Freud's extraordinary scientific achievement."

About the Author and Artist

Stephen Wilson qualified as a doctor in 1968 and subsequently specialized in psychiatry at Fulbourn Hospital, Cambridge, and the Littlemore and Warneford Hospitals in Oxford, where he was Honorary Senior Clinical Lecturer in the University Department of Psychiatry. He is also Honorary Research Fellow at the Centre for Psychoanalytic Studies, University of Kent, Canterbury. His publications include *Sigmund Freud* (1997), *The Cradle of Violence: Essays on Psychiatry, Psychoanalysis and Literature* (1995) and the forthcoming *The Bloomsbury Book of the Mind*. Dr Wilson is a practising psychotherapist and a Fellow of the Royal College of Psychiatrists, Consultant Psychotherapist at the Northampton Healthcare Trust, and Honorary Consulting Psychotherapist to the Oxfordshire Mental Healthcare Trust.

Oscar Zarate has illustrated many books in this series, including *Introducing Freud*, *Introducing Melanie Klein* and *Introducing Psychoanalysis*.

Acknowledgements from the Author

I should like to thank Ivan Ward for suggesting I do this, Sabina Strich for generously translating Alfred Hoche's 1910 paper and David Jones for referring me to Freud's views on homosexuality. Thanks are also due to Richard Appignanesi and Oscar Zarate, who transformed the text into something exciting and quite new. I continue to value Kate Wilson's criticism, which I am slowly learning to accept.

Index